SERGE IT
IN AN
HOUR
OR LESS

OTHER BOOKS AVAILABLE FROM CHILTON

ABCs of Serging, by Tammy Young and Lori Bottom

Distinctive Serger Gifts & Crafts, by Naomi Baker and Tammy Young

Gail Brown's All-New Instant Interiors, by Gail Brown

Innovative Serging, by Gail Brown and Tammy Young

The New Creative Serging Illustrated: The Complete Guide to Decorative Overlock Sewing, by Pati Palmer, Gail Brown, and Sue Green

A New Serge in Wearable Art, by Ann Boyce

No-Sew, Low-Sew Interior Decor, by Janis Bullis

No-Sew Special Effects, by Donna Albert

Serged Garments in Minutes, by Tammy Young and Naomi Baker

Serge a Simple Project, by Tammy Young and Naomi Baker

Serge Something Super for Your Kids, by Cindy Cummins

Sew & Serge Pillows! Pillows! Pillows!, by Jackie Dodson and Jan Saunders

Sew & Serge Terrific Textures, by Jackie Dodson and Jan Saunders

Quick Napkin Creations, by Gail Brown

The Ultimate Serger Answer Guide: Troubleshooting for any Overlock Brand or Model, by Naomi Baker, Gail Brown, and Cindy Kacynski

SERGE IT
IN AN
HOUR
OR LESS

Cindy Cummins

Chilton
BOOK COMPANY
Radnor, Pennsylvania

Designed by Melissa Ann Renfroe for GGS, Inc.
Cover design by Anthony Jacobson
Cover photos by Donna Chiarelli
Illustrations by Laurie Osborne and Selma Theiss Thole
Interior photos by Ray Marklin

Library of Congress Cataloging-in-Publication Data

Cummins, Cindy
    Serge it in an hour or less/Cindy Cummins
      p. cm.
    Includes index.
    ISBN 0-8019-8773-3
    1. Serging.   2. Clothing and dresses.   3. House furnishings.
    I. Title.
TT713.C84   1996   96-8945
646.2′044—dc20   CIP

Manufactured in the United States of America

1 2 3 4 5 6 7 8 9 0   5 4 3 2 1 0 9 8 7 6

To every working woman.

My hope is that the time saved by using *Serge It In An Hour or Less* will enable you to spend more time on things most precious: family and friends.

CONTENTS

CHAPTER 9

CELEBRATIONS

FOREWORD

My sewing motto in recent years has been "If I can't make it in a weekend, I simply won't do it." And I've had to stick to that, due in main part to my family priorities, plus career and community commitments. No one—especially me—wants the makings of my creative visions (these include fabrics, threads, patterns, notions, and notes, plus a consumed mindset) strewn throughout our home for more than a day or so.

When Cindy told me about her new book, the concept of a one-hour project (actually dozens) sounded right up my alley. Her style of conceptualizing clever serger projects has impressed me for many years and inspired me on several occasions to get serging. But this book stands apart. Cindy not only has provided us with forty-five attractive, usable, and interesting items to serge, but has done the most time-consuming part of any sewing/serging project for us: figuring materials, yardages, and, most important, serger adjustments. So we can simply shop (or raid the stash) and serge.

Enjoy the photos for fabric and color ideas and Cindy's brief but complete instructions and accompanying illustrations, then make these items for yourself or as gifts for friends and family. People won't believe how busy-you could find time to serge such splendid designs.

I praise Cindy's creativity, tenacity, and especially her serging prowess for giving us—busy, over-committed, yet creative women of the '90s—hope for indulging our creativity and using that precious serger. Whether you're making decorator Wall Pockets (Chapter Five) for a child's bedroom or Folding Chair Caps (Chapter Six) to quickly spiff up some dated card-table chairs for a bridal shower luncheon or bridge club, know with certainty you can do it in an hour or less. Thank you, Cindy.

Cindy Kacynski

Coauthor of *The Ultimate Serger Answer Guide*
(Chilton Book Company, 1996)

ACKNOWLEDGMENTS

I owe a debt of gratitude to the many companies and individuals that helped to make *Serge It In An Hour or Less* possible. In an effort to say "Thank You" and recognize each individually . . .

My husband, Steve, and children, Allyce, 9, and Jonathan, 4, for all of the time with me given up because of "*the* book." Thanks for understanding and keeping our household under some semblance of order.

My mom, Carol, for keeping Jonathan while I worked. Without her, and his preschool, there would be no time to write.

My dad, computer guru and overall empathizer. To him go highest praises, especially for showing me that "Alt.-Tab" thing in Windows. (One of these days I'll learn how to really use this computer!)

Ray Marklin, for his keen artistic ability and expert photography, and to Selma Thole and Laurie Osborne, for their clear and accurate portrayal of the how-to illustrations. Anyone who has seen my scrawled renderings and notes would understand that a tremendous amount of praise should be lavished on these two women (both working moms too).

The sewing machine companies that provide me with their latest model sewing machines and sergers and their related accessories: New Home Sewing Machine Co., Pfaff American Sales, Babylock, Elna, and Viking/White Sewing Machine Co.

Cindy Kacynski, former Serger Udate editor, fellow author, and mom of two young girls, for her undying support and understanding of delayed deadlines and for sending me PME (positive mental energy!) at times when I really needed it.

My fellow sewing professionals, for their ideas, input, and inspiration: Gail Brown, Diana Cedolia, Becky Gilbert, Carola Russell, and, especially, Jan Saunders, for her continual exchange of ideas and feedback, and, most of all, for being able to relate directly to the joys and frustrations of the working-at-home-with-young-children role.

And anyone I have not mentioned individually: Thank you for your help, kind words, interest, and PME; your generosity has not gone unnoticed.

The following are registered trademark names used in this book: *Burmilana, Candlelight, Craft Fuse, Decor 6, Decor 12, Designer 6, Dritz Threadfuse, FS Jewel, Fabri Tac, Fasturn, Glamour Thread, GlissenGloss, HeatNBond, Horizontal Thread Holder, Janome Acrylic Thread, Lycra, Maxi-Lock, Ombre, Pearl Crown Rayon Thread, Rayon Mez Alcazar Thread, Reflection, Ribbon Floss, Ribbon Thread, Success Acrylic Serging Yarn, Sulky Metallic, Sulky Rayon, Sulky Silver, Sulky Tear Easy, Metalfil, Stiffen Stuff, Styrofoam, Supersheen, Supertwist, Vario Plus Snap Kit, Ultrasheen, Velcro,* and *YKK.*

INTRODUCTION

Welcome to *Serge It In An Hour or Less*, and, yes, you really can! This book was written for those of you, like me, who are short on time, but long on intention. As a mother of two young children, and a typical procrastinator, my sewing/serging time is always at a premium. Out of necessity, I have come up with ways to shortcut the sewing/serging process in order to create a finished item. Serging something from start to finish in an hour not only is a boon to the ego, with instant serging gratification, but frees up time to spend with my friends and family, ultimately so that I can "have it all." I hope you will find that using *Serge It In An Hour or Less* will help you to do the same. To guide you through the set-up of this book, let me give you a quick tour through the contents:

♦ Serger Review—Shows several stitch formations and explains some basic serging techniques.

♦ Serging Tips and Shortcuts from the Pros—Contributions from the best sewing/serging experts in the field. Relax and browse through this section; you're sure to pick up an idea or two.

♦ Fifty Complete, One-Hour (or less) Serger Projects—Fully illustrated, with several photographed in full color.

♦ Patterns for Projects—Can be copied and/or enlarged on a photocopy machine.

♦ Resource Information—Given for many of the companies that provided their materials for this book. Check with them for local retailers or mail-order information.

♦ About the Author—Please write to me at the address listed with your comments, suggestions, tips, techniques, and ideas. I love hearing from each of you!

All of these projects are fast and easy to serge and are perfect to use as class teaching projects. One more bonus to serging these one-hour projects is that each allows you to try out a different decorative thread or technique on a sure-hit, super-fast project.

Enough said . . . get reading . . . then get serging!

Happy Serging!

Cindy Cummins

SERGER REVIEW

Fig. I-1

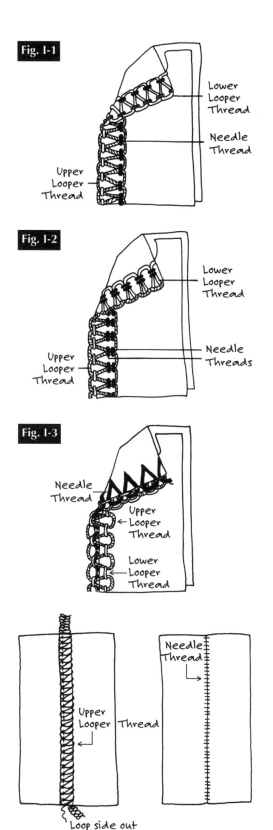

Lower Looper Thread

Needle Thread

Upper Looper Thread

Fig. I-2

Lower Looper Thread

Needle Threads

Upper Looper Thread

Fig. I-3

Needle Thread

Upper ← Looper Thread

Lower ← Looper Thread

Upper Looper Thread

Needle Thread

Loop side out

This is a review of basic serging stitches and techniques. It is intended as a reference guide to the stitches used in the projects shown in Chapters 2 through 9 of this book.

BASIC SERGER STITCHES

3-Thread Overlock—Use one needle and upper and lower loopers (Fig. I-1).

3/4-Thread Overlock—Use two needles and upper and lower loopers (Fig. I-2).

3-Thread Flatlock—Use one needle and upper and lower loopers. Loosen needle tension and slightly tighten lower looper tension (Fig. I-3).

2-Thread Flatlock—Use one needle and lower looper. Loosen needle tension and slightly tighten lower looper tension (Fig. I-4).

Rolled Hem—May be 2- or 3-thread stitch. Use one needle and lower looper for 2-thread rolled hem. Use one needle and upper and lower loopers for 3-thread rolled hem. Loosen upper looper tension and tighten lower looper tension for 3-thread rolled hem (Figs. I-5 and I-6).

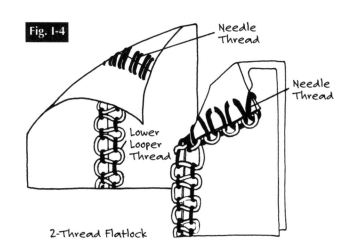

Fig. I-4

Needle Thread

Needle Thread

Lower Looper Thread

2-Thread Flatlock

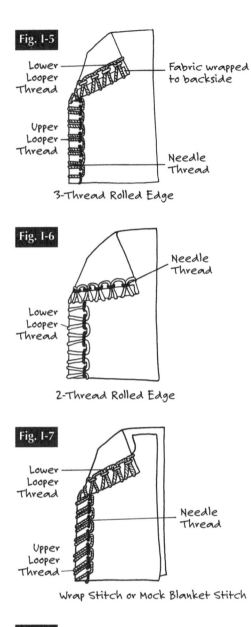

Fig. I-5

Lower Looper Thread

Fabric wrapped to backside

Upper Looper Thread

Needle Thread

3-Thread Rolled Edge

Fig. I-6

Needle Thread

Lower Looper Thread

2-Thread Rolled Edge

Fig. I-7

Lower Looper Thread

Needle Thread

Upper Looper Thread

Wrap Stitch or Mock Blanket Stitch

Fig. I-8

Looper Thread

Needle Thread

Cover Stitch

Wrapped Stitch—Use one needle and upper and lower loopers. Similar to rolled hem, but fabric edge is not rolled within stitch. Loosen upper looper tension and tighten lower looper tension (Fig. I-7).

Cover Stitch—Use two needles and lower looper or chain-stitch looper (depending on serger make and model). Results in two parallel lines of stitching on top side and loop configuration on underside. The cutting blade is disengaged, and stitches can be formed on the edge or within fabric (Fig. I-8).

Differential Feed—This feed mechanism (available on many sergers) is most commonly used to ease the edge of fabric to help prevent stretching or "wavy" edges, or to pull the fabric taut to eliminate puckering. Two sets of feed dogs are adjusted to ease or pull the fabric taut as it is being serged. Can also be used at a high setting to gather fabric or at a low setting to lettuce fabric.

SECURING STITCHES

Seam Sealant—Use a drop of seam sealant at the ends of serger stitching (Fig. I-9). Let dry, then clip off excess chain. Always test seam sealant on scrap fabric and decorative threads before using on actual project.

Burying Tail Chain—Use a tapestry (large blunt-tip) needle or double-eyed needle to pull the excess chain back through the serging (Fig. I-10). Clip off excess chain.

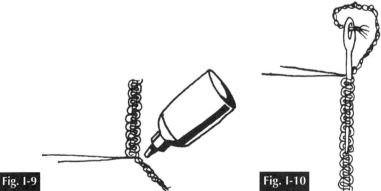

Fig. I-9

Fig. I-10

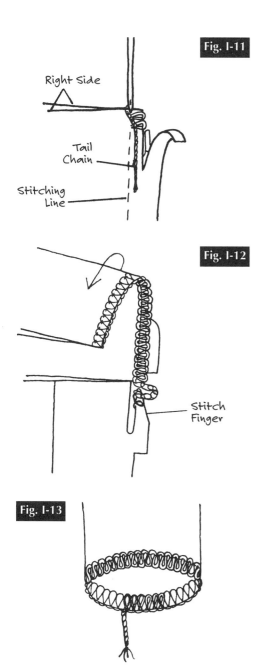

Fig. I-11

Right Side

Tail Chain

Stitching Line

Fig. I-12

Stitch Finger

Fig. I-13

Serge over Chain—At the beginning of a seam, take a stitch into the fabric. Raise presser foot, then pull tail chain to front under presser foot. Lower presser foot, serge over chain for approximately 1″ and let knife cut away excess chain (Fig. I-11).

Flip and Stitch—At the end of a seam, take one stitch off fabric. Raise presser foot and clear stitch finger. Turn fabric over and place back under presser foot. Lower presser foot and serge for 1/2″ to 1″, then gradually serge off the edge (Fig. I-12).

Overlap Stitches—A method of securing stitches on a continuous seam. Start serging in the middle of a long edge, preferably not on a curve. Stop serging when the knife meets beginning stitches. If possible disengage the upper knife. Continue serging, taking care not to cut the beginning stitches (if the knife cannot be disengaged), overlapping approximately two to six stitches. Overlap fewer stitches for heavy threads, more for finer threads. Clear stitch finger, then chain off. Bury or tie the tail threads or chain to the wrong side (Fig. I-13). Often used for serging-in-the-round.

Speed Serging

Serging Tips and Shortcuts— From the Pros

Are you short on time? At your wit's end with your serger? Need a neat trick to inspire you? Here's some help—super serger tips and techniques from the best serger-sewers in the industry. I have also included several of my favorite tips. Take it easy, grab a cup of coffee (or whatever your preference), and read on.

BEFORE YOU SERGE

"One of the best investments I ever made for my sewing room is an adjustable computer-style chair with good back support, air-lift mechanism, and wheels. I have my sewing/serging area set up in a U shape and can wheel back and forth between sewing machines, sergers, and pressing area with little effort." Cindy

"Keep handled thread snips handy at your serger by hanging them from inexpensive little suction-cup hooks adhered to the side of your machine. Suction-cup hooks are readily available in craft and fabric stores." Cindy Kacynski, coauthor of *The Ultimate Serger Answer Guide— Troubleshooting For Any Overlock Brand or Model* (Fig. 1-1)

Fig. 1-1 Keep thread snips handy with suction-cup hooks adhered to the side of your machine.

"Ever feel all thumbs when changing your serger needle? Use a locking needle gripper to securely hold the needle so it won't fall into the machine. This leaves one hand free to tighten the screw." Judy Drury & Judy Kessinger (Judes'), sewing instructors and authors

"When first learning to thread your serger, or if you are having difficulty perfecting a stitch, thread the machine with the colors of thread that match the color-coded thread guides (on most sergers). You will easily be able to distinguish between needles and loopers for correct adjustment." Cindy

"Cut a 6″ square of fabric from each of your sewing projects, and stack them in a small box next to your serger. Whenever you readjust your machine for different stitches, techniques, fabrics, or thread types, you'll have a variety of fabric types on hand for easy test-serging." Cindy Kacynski, coauthor of *The Ultimate Serger Answer Guide—Troubleshooting for Any Overlock Brand or Model* (Fig. 1-2)

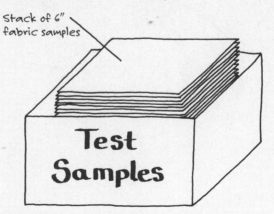

Stack of 6″ fabric samples

Test Samples

Fig. 1-2 Cut 6″-squares from scraps of sewing projects and stack in a small box next to your serger for use as test samples.

"Thread clips are a necessity when serging. I keep mine on a neon-colored ribbon to wear around my neck. When I remove them, the bright color makes them easier to find on my cluttered project table." Cindy

"I use my serger for decorative edge work on occasion, and as a timesaver I keep a file box of samples with the exact serger settings, thread type, and any helpful hints I found to work based on previous experience. When I want to recreate an edge, I start where I was successful last time and fine-tune the settings depending on the fabric type." Linda Turner Griepentrog, editor, *Sew News*

"Dental floss threaders make great looper threaders and are inexpensive. Place thread through loop, then pass end through looper eye. Look for these in the toothbrush section of any drugstore." Cindy

"One thing that is essential in the sequence of threading: The needles must be threaded after the lower looper. Serger manuals instruct you to cut the needle threads and rethread the needles after threading the lower looper. This isn't necessary; Instead, gently drag the tweezers under the raised presser foot, pulling the needle threads up from around the looper and back under the presser foot." Judy Barlup, sewing instructor and producer of video *Japanese Tailoring*

"Occasionally when you purchase a piece of fabric, there may be some difficulty in determining which is the right and wrong side. It may be apparent while on your cutting table, but not after it's been through the washer and dryer. To assist with this, I serge the raw edges, right side up, with white thread in the upper looper and a dark color in the lower looper. This does two things: Light = right side (right rhymes with light), and by looking at the white thread, you can determine if this fabric is colorfast." Donna Hoeflinger, American Sewing Guild, Houston (Fig. 1-3)

"Before starting to serge, open your looper cover and take a quick glance at each thread path—from thread cone or spool to needle or looper eye. Are any threads mispositioned or caught on an obstruction? Then give each thread a gentle tug above and below each tension disc to ensure it's engaged. The thirty seconds it takes to do this will save you hours of frustration later." Cindy Kacynski, coauthor of *The Ultimate Serger Answer Guide—Troubleshooting for Any Overlock Brand or Model*

"Use thread nets on cones or spools of unruly thread, or when a bit of extra tension is needed. The easiest way to use a thread net is to place one end of it up through the bottom of the cone, pushing most of the net inside, then pull out amount of net that is needed to wrap up and over the cone. This controls the excess net so it will not catch on the thread as it feeds from the top of the cone. And when the cone is placed on the thread spindle, the thread net stays put." Cindy (Fig. 1-4)

Fig. 1-4 Place end of thread net up through bottom of cone, then pull out amount needed to wrap up and over the cone of thread.

"One of my favorite serging tools is my pair of reverse tweezers. Instead of coming together when they are depressed, these tweezers open, then firmly clamp down when released. These are especially great for threading decorative thread through the

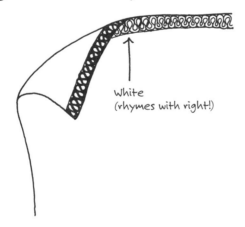

White
(rhymes with right!)

Fig. 1-3 Serge-finish fabric with white thread on right side, dark thread on wrong side.

loopers. The thread stays clamped in the tweezers even with unsteady hands." Jan Saunders, author of *Jan Saunders' Wardrobe Quick-Fixes,* coauthor of *Sew and Serge Terrific Textures, Sew and Serge Pillows! Pillows! Pillows!,* and nine other sewing and serging books

"Even though I have a thread catcher of some sort for all of my sergers, I find that a gallon-size clear plastic bag taped in a convenient place at my sewing table, is perfect for disposing excess threads and sewing trash. This way I can toss threads and snippets before they land on my sewing room floor (to be ultimately tangled in the vacuum beater bar). The clear bag lets me see when I need to empty it before it overflows!" Cindy

WHILE YOU SERGE

"Continuously feed pieces to be serged through the machine, without stopping to cut the chain in-between, saving thread and time!" L.J. Aikin, serger enthusiast and America Online contributor (Fig. 1-5)

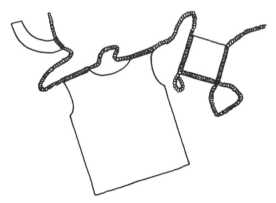

Fig. 1-5 Continuously feed several pieces of a project through the serger without stopping to cut chains.

"When gathering on your serger, use a different color thread in the needle. It makes it much easier to find the needle thread if you need more gathers." Diana Cedolia, freelance sewing educator

"To create perfect points on sheer or very lightweight fabrics, use a press-on-type fabric stabilizer on the corners only. Serge corner as usual, then tear excess stabilizer away. Any amount left within the stitch will come out in the wash." Cindy

"When I am roll-edging a heavier or loosely woven fabric, or one that's just plain difficult to roll, I drop

my right needle and employ the left to create a wider bite, which rolls the fabric much easier with no 'pokeys' sticking out (some sergers can't roll-edge with the left needle—check your serger manual for stitch capabilities). The results are a little wider, but no less attractive." Marilyn Gatz, designer and sewing lecturer and educator

"If I'm having a problem with the serger, rather than continue to frustrate myself, I walk away for fifteen minutes and then come back with a refreshed perspective. Usually I'm able to solve the problem much quicker than if I'd agonized over it without a break." Linda Turner Griepentrog, editor, *Sew News* (Fig. 1-6)

Fig. 1-6 When serger frustration gets you down, take a fifteen-minute break. Upon returning, you can usually solve the problem much quicker.

"When estimating the amount of decorative thread needed for a project, try using this formula:

> ***BALANCED SERGING***
> Loopers—10 × length to be serged
>
> ***ROLLED-EDGE/WRAPPED STITCH***
> Upper looper—10 × length to be serged
>
> ***FLATLOCKING***
> Needle—10 × length to be serged
> Upper looper—10 × length to be serged

Remember, these are only estimates. Be sure to add extra for test serging and mistakes!" Naomi Baker, coauthor of *The Ultimate Serger Answer Guide, Craft an Elegant Wedding,* and several other sewing and serging books

"Make your own piping with a rolled edge by simply serging over a filler onto a strip of bias-cut fabric.

Leave a 1/2″ lip to insert into your seam. This is a great place to use heavier and decorative threads for beautiful effects." Karen Kunkel, editor, designer, and consultant to the home sewing industry (Fig. 1-7)

Fig. 1-7 Make perfectly coordinated piping by serging a rolled hem with decorative thread on folded edge of bias strip.

"When I serge with several strands of thread in the upper looper (thread blending), I run about half of the strands through the tension disc of the unused needle. This really helps to make the threads lie smoothly, especially if they are different thickness." Diana Cedolia, freelance sewing educator

"To reduce bulk at intersecting seams, press the seams in opposite directions before joining. This will help the serger feed the seam more evenly and will eliminate skipped stitches from serging over a 'hump' of seam allowances." Cindy

"If your serger is equipped with cover stitch capabilities, try using the cover stitch as a mock flatlock stitch. This is achieved by placing decorative thread in the looper and stitching with the wrong side up. This stitch looks similar to a flatlock stitch but actually lies much flatter. The design possibilities are endless and fun!" Susie Parker, training consultant, Bernina of America

"When adjusting for a satin stitch using heavier thread, begin testing at a medium-length stitch and shorten the stitch to perfect it. If you begin with the length too short, the thread can jam under the presser foot." Tammy Young, coauthor of *ABC's of Serging,* author of *The Crafter's Guide to Glues,* and twelve other sewing and serging books

FAVORITE TECHNIQUES

"A rolled-hem stitch works beautifully for narrow, inconspicuous seams on sheer and lace fabrics. Use a 2- or 3-thread narrow rolled edge, lightweight thread, and a stitch length of 1.5mm–2mm, serging

with fabric right sides together." Karen Kunkel, editor, designer, and consultant to the home sewing industry

"Use clear elastic to stabilize seams (particularly shoulder and neckline seams on stretch-prone sweaterknits and other knits). Simply serge over it without stretching. It's super soft and lightweight, so it won't add bulk or cause wearing discomfort." Cindy Kacynski, coauthor of *The Ultimate Serger Answer Guide—Troubleshooting for Any Overlock Brand or Model* (Fig. 1-8)

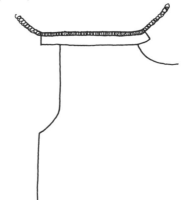

Fig. 1-8 Use clear elastic to stabilize seams and add a bit of give.

"If you are having difficulties with the 'pokeys' on ravel-prone fabrics, try double-serge-finishing the edge. First, serge the edge with a narrow, medium-length stitch. Then, set serger for a medium to wide, satin-length stitch to cover the first line of serging. Take care not to trim the edge during the second serge, for neat covered edges." Gail Brown, coauthor of *The Ultimate Serger Answer Guide,* author of *Gail Brown's All-New Instant Interiors,* and several other sewing and serging books

"Add a delicate touch to the ribbing on a T-shirt by lettucing each side of the ribbing. Cut the ribbing as usual, set serger for rolled hem, and stretch

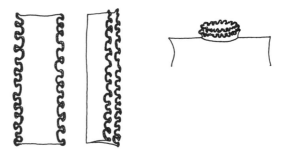

Fig. 1-9 Add a delicate touch to ribbing by lettucing each side of ribbing.

the ribbing firmly but gently while you serge-finish the long edges. Serge the ribbing in a circle, fold, off-setting the edges, and apply the folded edge to the neckline or sleeves." Judy Barlup, sewing instructor, producer of video *Japanese Tailoring* (Fig. 1-9)

"For a two-toned ribbed neck and sleeve:

1 Cut the outer crew strip 1 1/4″ wide by a 3:4 ratio of the neck measurement. Cut sleeve and lower band strips 2″ wide by 3:4 ratio.

2 Cut the inner rib strip 1 7/8″ wide and the same length as the outer strip. Cut sleeve and lower band strips 2 5/8″ wide and the same length as the outer strip.

3 With right sides together, serge the strips along one long edge. Finger-press the seam allowance toward the wider inner rib.

4 Straight stitch the short rib ends together, forming a tube; finger-press the seam open.

5 Fold the combined strips in half lengthwise; the wider inner rib strip will fold around the raw edge of the narrow outer strip forming a 1/4″ stripe along the folded edge.

6 Quarter the rib and the garment. Serge the rib to the garment with the outer rib next to the garment right side."

Sallie J. Russell, designer, author, and sewing instructor

"Serge over a filler cord for a decorative finish on formal wear garments to hem ruffled edges. Use fishline #10 weight or fine wire (used for jewelry and beadwork) as a filler. Place the filler between your needle and upper knife blade and serge over the top, onto the fabric, incorporating the filler within the stitch." Karen Kunkel, editor, designer, and consultant to the home sewing industry

"Recycle and renew ravel-edged towels using double-serged edges (see Gail Brown's tip on ravel-prone fabrics) and woolly stretch nylon thread. Set serger for a wrapped stitch, with woolly stretch nylon thread in loopers and needle. The thread will fluff out after serging and add strength and durability to the finished edge." Cindy

"Corded tubes are great for making beefy tie and frog closures. Cut fine cable or satin cord (1/4″

diameter or smaller) twice the strip length, plus 2–3″. Fold the fabric strip in half lengthwise, right sides together, sandwiching the cord within the fold. Serge the seam, then secure the tube to the cord midpoint by straight stitching across the tube end. Pull the cord to turn the tube right side out and fill at the same time." Gail Brown, coauthor of *The Ultimate Serger Answer Guide,* author of *Gail Brown's All-New Instant Interiors,* and several other sewing and serging books

HAPPY ENDINGS

"Form a knot for a very secure serger tail inside a garment or project where the end does not show. Follow these steps:

1 Pull the fullness out of the serger chain with your fingers, starting at the fabric edge.

2 Trim the chain to 3–4″ for ease in tying.

3 Make a loop with the chain. Pull the tail end of the chain through the loop. Tweezers make this easier. Place a pin at the edge of the fabric (Fig. 1-10).

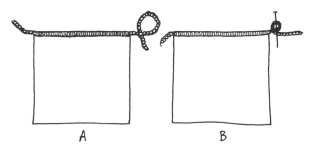

Fig. 1-10 Make a chain knot close to fabric edge by using a pin to guide thread loop.

4 Pull the loop tight against the pin.

5 Remove the pin. Push the knot tight against the fabric with your thumbnail.

6 Clip the end, leaving 1/4–1/2″. Seam sealant can be added if you feel the need."

Sue Barnabee, editorial assistant, *Serger Update*

"When using a tapestry needle to pull the thread tail through the serger stitches, start about an inch away from the thread tail and run the eye of the needle (unthreaded) through the stitches toward the end. Then thread the tail chain through the needle eye and pull through. Even a very short thread tail can be buried and secured in this manner." Judy Barlup, sewing instructor and producer of video *Japanese Tailoring*

"After burying the tail chain through the last inch of threads, I like to add a little extra security by making a second loop through the last stitch (where the tail chain exits). This helps to keep the buried chain from slipping out, especially on slick-surface fabrics." Cindy

Timesaving Notions and Accessories

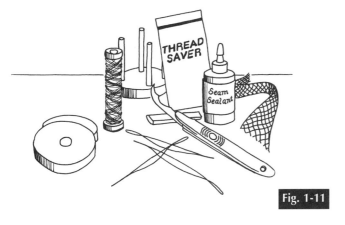

Fig. 1-11

These are the serging notions and "helpers" that I find myself reaching for time and time again. Using these practical—and often indispensable—items can cut your serging time (as well as frustration level) dramatically. Most can be found at your local retailer, but if availability is a problem, check out some of the great mail-order companies listed at the back of this book.

Double-eyed Needle—This "needle" has a large eye at each end. It is a bit longer than a traditional tapestry needle, making it easier to handle when burying tail chains.

HeatNBond Lite—This is a great fusible adhesive. In contrast to a fusible web, this product gives total coverage without bubbling. Be sure to get the Lite version of this product for serging, as the regular version is no-sew.

Horizontal Thread Holder—A great helper when using decorative threads that should be fed from the side instead of the top to prevent twisting. Sits on a thread spindle to hold a spool horizontal-

ly instead of vertically. Especially useful when serging with foil-type threads such as Sulky Sliver and Glissen Gloss Prizm.

Instant Ripper—I find this to be a neat little tool. Its plastic comfort handle and sharp ripping blade let you glide easily through serged stitches when reverse sewing is required.

Needle/Looper Threader—I use this notion on a daily basis. These threaders are constructed from a very fine gauge wire, forming a loop, that is fused together at one end. The result is a threader that will pass easily through looper eyes as well as needles too. A small twist at the loop end keeps the thread secured in place and will not slip out when the threader is accidentally dropped.

Nonstick Pressing Sheet—I put this sheet down on my pressing surface when fusing anything. The residue collects on the pressing sheet, rather than on my muslin blocking board, and will peel off easily once cooled. You may also use this as an actual pressing cloth, pressing directly on the sheet's surface with the iron.

Polyester monofilament-nylon thread—This miracle thread is truly wonderful. Very fine, like other invisible monofilaments, this variety is made from 100% polyester, so it can withstand more heat than 100% nylon varieties. Use this thread in the needles or loopers depending on the desired decorative result. It also makes a great invisible topstitch thread for serger appliqué.

Reverse Tweezers—A must-have notion for fumble fingered serger-sewers like myself. These ingenious tweezers are perfect for guiding decorative thread through loopers. Working in reverse when the tweezers are squeezed, the pointed tips open up to grab the thread; when released they clamp closed.

Seam Sealant—Another one of those indispensable products for serging, this gluelike substance can be used on tail chains to keep them from fraying. Place one drop of seam sealant near the base of the seam, let dry, then snip away excess chain. Always test sealant on scrap fabric and thread to check for colorfastness and so forth.

Spool Rings—These foam rings sit on the base of your serger thread stand, helping reduce static and backspin on unruly threads. They can also help keep the thread from slipping under the spool or cone where it ultimately gets tangled.

Thread Nets—Place these over cones or spools of thread to help prevent backspin or to add a bit of tension on the thread. Place the condensed thread net up through the bottom of the cone, then flip the net up and over the edge of the cone, pulling just the right amount of net to cover the cone.

Thread Palette—This little device is used to hold up to four different threads for thread blending. The small round platform is positioned on one of your serger's thread spindles, and features four pegs to hold additional threads. Threads feed evenly from the palette, through either upper or lower looper, for fun, decorative effects.

Thread Saver—A clear, vinyl sheet, cut to fit thread cones and spools, that clings to itself when wrapped around. These are great for keeping threads from becoming a tangled mess; and can also be used in lieu of a thread net when wrapped loosely around rayon threads.

Decorative Threads

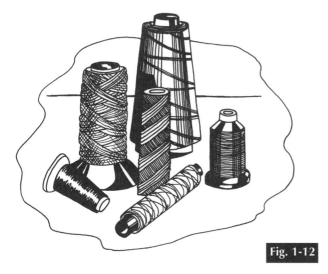

Fig. 1-12

A myriad of decorative threads are on the market today. This listing is intended as a guide to those threads and their uses. Companies are constantly adding new and wonderful threads to their lines, so be on the lookout for more new offerings.

Decorative threads are either cross-wound, for even feeding off the top of the cone or tube, or parallel-wound, with the thread feeding from the side of the spool. Use a thread or spool cap for small tubes or parallel-wound spools to keep the thread from tangling before reaching the thread guides.

Thread nets and spool rings are also a great help to keep slippery threads (that tend to unwind or backspin) under control.

HEAVY DECORATIVE THREADS

These threads are sometimes classified as yarns because of their weight. Heavy decorative threads stand out against fabric edges and can create braid-like effects when a shorter stitch length is used. All of these heavy decorative threads work well in the upper and/or lower looper, but they are usually too heavy to use in the needle. I have included (in parentheses) the manufacturer's name. Check the resource listing for more information.

Candlelight—A soft, smooth, heavy metallic thread/yarn. Several solid and variegated colors (YLI Corp.).

Glamour—Smooth, moderately twisted thread, 65% viscose, 35% metallic polyester. Several solid and variegated colors (SCS-Madeira).

Janome Acrylic—A softly twisted 100% acrylic thread with a high sheen. Several colors (New Home Company).

Jeans Stitch—A midweight 100% spun polyester thread originally intended as topstitching thread. Has a matte finish and is perfect for serging. Several colors (YLI Corp.).

Ombre—A softly twisted eight-ply heavy metallic yarn. Several solid and variegated colors (Kreinik Mfg.).

Pearl Cotton—A 100% mercerized cotton thread. Comes in three sizes: 5 (heaviest), 8, and 12 (finest). Put up on balls that may be wound by hand onto an empty cone for serger use. Large array of colors (Coats & Clark, DMC, others).

Pearl Crown Rayon—A twisted 100% rayon thread with a high sheen. Many colors (YLI Corp.).

Ribbon Floss—A 100% rayon braided mini-ribbon with a lustrous sheen. Many colors; also some metallics (Rhode Island Textile Co.).

Success Acrylic Serging Yarn—A 100% acrylic yarn with a wool-like texture. Several basic colors (YLI Corp.).

Burmilana—A 30% wool, 70% acrylic yarn, with a fine wool texture. Several colors (SCS-Madeira).

Reflection—A #8 fine braided cord. Metallic finish. Several colors (Rhode Island Textile Co.).

HIGH-COVERAGE DECORATIVE THREADS

These threads may be light to heavy in weight, but each produces a filled-in look on serged stitches. Choose this type of thread when you need an edge completely covered, without any fabric peeking through between stitches. These threads may be placed in the loopers (Woolly Nylon may also be used in the needle).

Woolly Nylon—A heat-set crimped 100% nylon thread with a fuzzy hand, this soft yet very strong thread is great for comfortable, durable seams on kids' clothes, swim wear, and aerobic wear, as well as for decorative edges. Great in upper looper for rolled-edge satin stitch. There are two weights: Woolly nylon and woolly nylon extra (three times the loftiness). Huge selection of colors (YLI Corp., similar products by Swiss-Metrosene, Talon, and others).

Designer 6—A slightly twisted 100% rayon filament thread (the twist adds durability) with a super-high sheen. Many colors (YLI Corp.).

Decor 6—A very lightly twisted 100% rayon filament thread with a bright high sheen. Many colors (SCS-Madeira).

FINE DECORATIVE THREADS

These decorative threads are relatively easy to use and can be placed in the needles and the loopers.

Fine Rayon—A 100% viscose rayon embroidery thread. Has a lustrous sheen and works beautifully in upper looper to create pretty rolled edges. Two common weights, 30 wt. and 40 wt., with 30 wt. being the heavier of the two (Sulky of America, A & E, Coats & Clark, Pfaff, and others).

Fine Acrylic—A 100% acrylic embroidery thread. Has a shiny finish and is very strong (YLI Corp., New Home Company, others).

Conventional Serger Cone Thread—Can be 100% polyester or cotton-covered polyester. This basic serger thread is considered decorative when used in any serger application where the thread is exposed. Very easy to use; try placing extra cones on cone thread stands and threading two threads at a time through the loopers for heavier coverage.

Comes in a virtually limitless array of colors and varieties (A & E, Coats & Clark, Swiss-Metrosene, Talon, and others).

FINE METALLIC THREADS

These threads are finer and lighter in weight than their heavier counterparts. As a result, they may fray when used in the lower looper or needle. For best results, use a Metafil or machine embroidery needle if your serger accepts conventional sewing machine needles (also called household needles) to help reduce thread breakage. Although sometimes "testy" to use, these metallics are just the thing for shiny holiday rolled edges and for glitzy flatlocking on lightweight fabrics.

Coats & Clark Metallic—This fine metallic thread has a polyester core that is twisted with a metallic wrap. Several colors (Coats & Clark).

FS Jewel—This metallic thread is a blend of 80% rayon, 20% polyester metallic, resulting in a bold, slightly beefy texture. Several solid and variegated colors (Madeira USA).

Sulky Metallic—A fine metallic thread with a polyester core, wrapped by a fine metallic foil. Several solid and variegated colors (Sulky of America).

Sulky Sliver—A fine foil thread with a super high sheen. Use a Horizontal Threader Holder to prevent twisting or breakage of this thread (Sulky of America, similar products by SCS-Madeira, others).

Supertwist—A fine metallic thread consisting of two threads blended together for extra sparkle. Several solid and variegated colors (Madeira USA).

Woolly Nylon Metallic—This is the easiest of the fine metallics to use; the metallic foil is twisted with a core of woolly nylon. Basic colors (YLI Corp.).

SPECIALTY DECORATIVE THREADS

While the following threads may not be classified directly as decorative threads, they work in combination with other decorative threads to achieve specific results.

Nylon Monofilament—A soft, invisible, 100% nylon thread. Can be used in the needle as well as in the loopers. Great for difficult-to-match fabric or for flatlocking heavier threads or yarns onto garments. Clear and smoke "colors." (YLI Corp., Coats & Clark, and others).

Polyester Monofilament—A soft invisible 100% polyester thread. Can be used in the needle as well as in the loopers. Can accept more heat than 100% nylon monofilament (Sulky of America and SCS-Madeira).

Threadfuse—A polyester thread core wrapped with a fusible filament so that it bonds with the touch of an iron. Use in the lower looper to create a tight bond for serger appliqué, hems, or trims (Dritz).

Wash-Away Basting Thread—A filament thread that dissolves when placed in warm water. Use to create serged picot edges and other decorative effects (YLI Corp.).

Klassy Kids

Sneaker Peekers and Cool Laces

Fig. 2-1

Kids love these sneaker accessories. Serged from your scrap stash, sneaker peekers and matching shoelaces are a snap to make. Try customizing them to special outfits or in team colors, with painted or embroidered trim, for footwear decor that is sure to raise cheers from your favorite kid!

MATERIALS

Scraps of light- to medium-weight woven fabrics
One cone of decorative thread, such as Pearl
    Crown Rayon, Designer 6, or Decor 6
Three cones of serger thread
Seam sealant or clear nail polish
Transparent tape
Fabric paints
Embroidery thread

Serger Set-Up

For shoelaces: Medium-length rolled hem stitch, serger thread in loopers and needle.

For sneaker peekers: Satin-length, rolled-hem stitch, decorative thread in the upper looper, serger thread in the lower looper and needle.

Instructions

1 Cut four sneaker peekers from fabric scraps, using pattern number 1. Cut 1″-wide fabric strips for shoelaces the desired length (30″–36″ is standard for eight-eyelet sneakers).

2 Serge long edge of each lace strip, tapering off at ends to form a point. When serging second edge of piece, hold tail chain from previous serged edge taut behind serger presser foot to help keep from "chewing" fabric. Dot ends with seam sealant, let dry, then trim tail chain (Fig. 2-2).

Fig. 2-2

3 Wrap a 1″ piece of transparent tape tightly around seam-sealed ends (if tape is wrapped loosely, lace end will not fit through eyelet in shoe). Coat with seam sealant or clear nail polish and let dry. Repeat applications of sealant or polish until wrapped ends are hard (Fig. 2-3).

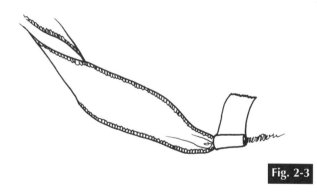

Fig. 2-3

4 Place two sneaker peeker pieces wrong sides together. Serge-finish all sides by serging short sides first, then upper and lower edges. Dot corners with seam sealant, let dry, then trim tail chains (Fig. 2-4). Repeat for the remaining two sneaker peeker pieces.

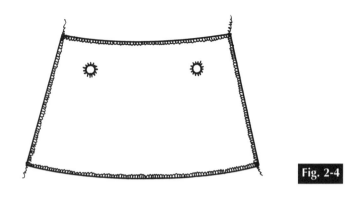

Fig. 2-4

5 Make eyelets or small buttonholes on both peekers according to pattern markings. Decorate one or both sides (these are reversible) with motif of your choice, using fabric paint, embroidery, or other decorative application.

6 Thread a laced, untied shoelace through each peeker, then tie laces into a bow, gathering the peeker slightly to give it a "kiltie" effect.

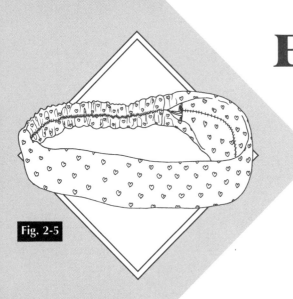

Fig. 2-5

Easy-Fit Headband

This stretchy headband can be easily adjusted to fit all sizes. Make one from Lycra knit for a decorative hair accessory or one from lofty polar fleece to keep ears toasty warm. Super quick and easy to serge, these headbands can be made to match every outfit.

MATERIALS

1/8 yard of Lycra knit *or* 1/4 yard of polar fleece
8″ of 3/4″-wide elastic
Three cones of woolly nylon thread

Serger Set-Up

Wide, 3-thread flatlock, medium-length stitch, woolly stretch nylon thread in loopers and needle.

Instructions

1 From Lycra cut one 4 1/2″ × 13″ rectangle and one 2 1/2″ × 12″ rectangle (if using polar fleece, cut larger rectangle 6″ × 13″).

2 Fold each rectangle in half lengthwise, right sides together. Serge-seam the long raw edge of each (Fig. 2-6).

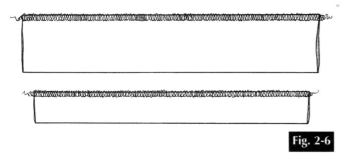

Fig. 2-6

3 Turn bands right side out, gently pulling flat-locking open. Insert elastic through the narrower band, centering seam along elastic. Stitch close to one end to secure band to elastic. Use a safety pin to secure band/elastic at opposite end (Fig. 2-7).

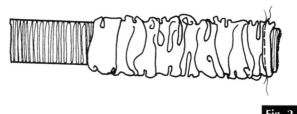

Fig. 2-7

4 Center flatlocked seam on wide band. Place stitched end of elasticized band to raw end of wide band, right sides together. Fold ends around elastic piece as shown, stitch to secure, trim end neatly, then fold band over end (Fig. 2-8).

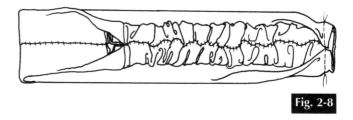

Fig. 2-8

5 Measure band around head. Adjust elastic to fit and trim away excess elastic. Stitch to secure wide band to elastic band and finish end as instructed in step 4.

Cowboy Bib

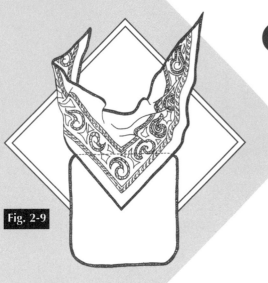

Fig. 2-9

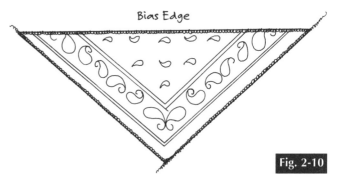

Bias Edge

Fig. 2-10

Little ones will finish their meals without a drop on their clothes thanks to this cute cowboy bib. Kids love this design and it's fun as well as practical. Use a bandana or bandana print for the kerchief, terry cloth or a purchased washcloth for the bib.

MATERIALS

20″ square of bandana print fabric or ready-made bandana
13″ square of terry cloth or a large washcloth
One cone of decorative thread, such as Sulky Rayon, Ultrasheen, or woolly nylon
Two cones serger thread

Serger Set-Up

Kerchief: Rolled hem, 3-thread, satin-length stitch, decorative thread in upper looper, serger thread in lower looper and needle.

Bib: Narrow, 3-thread, satin-length, balanced stitch, decorative thread in upper looper, serger thread in lower looper and needle.

Instructions

1 Cut the bandana print or bandana in half diagonally. Set one half aside to use for another bib. Round the corners of the terry square using a saucer.

2 Serge-finish the kerchief piece. Use differential feed across top bias edge to help prevent stretching (Fig. 2-10).

3 Serge-finish all sides of terry square. If using terry washcloth, trim away previous stitching, then serge-finish edges. To help prevent "pokeys," serge-finish edge twice, widening the second line of serging slightly and taking care not to cut the first row of serging (Fig. 2-11).

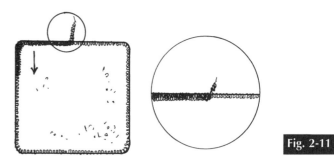

Fig. 2-11

4 Lap and edgestitch finished kerchief piece on terry square, as shown (Fig. 2-12).

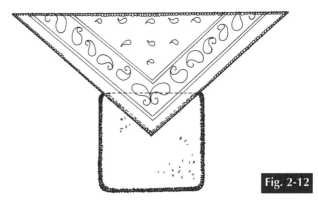

Fig. 2-12

5 Tie ends around child's neck, then smooth down folds.

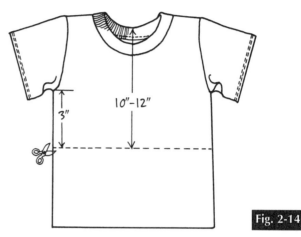

Fig. 2-13

Girl's Baby-Doll T-Shirt Dress

Fig. 2-14

Mothers love to see their daughters in dress-up clothes, but kids, more often than not, prefer more casual wear. To make both mothers and daughters happy, try serging this make-it-in-an-instant baby-doll style dress. Whether you use a ready-made T-shirt or serge your own, this comfortable-to-wear and easy-to-care-for dress will soon become a favorite.

MATERIALS

Ready-made T-shirt *or* interlock fabric and ribbing and favorite T-shirt pattern, amount according to pattern, less 1/4 yard
1 3/4 yards of coordinating 45"-wide lightweight shirting fabric
1 yard of 3/8"-wide clear elastic
Three to four cones serger thread

Serger Set-Up

Wide 3- or 4-thread, medium-length, balanced stitch, serger thread in loopers and needles.

Instructions

1 Cut out T-shirt from interlock and ribbing according to pattern instructions, shortening the T-shirt front and back to 3–4" below the underarm seam. If using a ready-made T-shirt, trim away excess T-shirt 3–4" below the underarm seam or 10"–12" from center back neck to lower edges (Fig. 2-14).

2 Construct T-shirt as per pattern instructions, utilizing flat serger construction order for T-shirts: Serge one shoulder seam, apply neckline ribbing, and serge remaining shoulder seam. Serge-finish and hem sleeves, serge sleeves to armholes, and serge underarm/side seams.

3 From the shirting fabric, cut two 45"-wide rectangles, each the desired dress length (skirt front and back). Right sides together, serge side seams (Fig. 2-15).

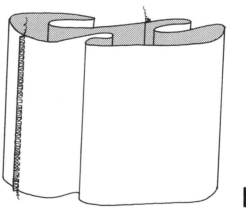

Fig. 2-15

4 Gather the upper edge of skirting as follows: Stretch the clear elastic a few times to prevent it from stretching too much during application. Measure T-shirt lower edge; cut elastic this length minus 2″. Quarter-mark the elastic and the skirting upper edge. Matching quarter-markings and stretching the elastic to fit, serge-seam the elastic to the skirting upper edge, wrong side, trimming a scant 1/4″ from the fabric (don't trim elastic) and catching the elastic in serging (Fig. 2-16).

5 With right sides together and side seams matching, serge the lower edge of T-shirt to upper edge of shirt without stretching the T-shirt.

6 Hem the skirting lower edge as desired.

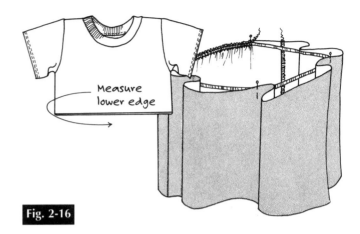

Measure lower edge

Fig. 2-16

Fig. 2-17

One-Piece Bloomin' Vest

from upper to lower edge, flatlock each stem, leaving excess chains.

TIP To ensure that flatlock pulls completely flat, allow serger stitches to fall halfway off folded edge (Fig. 2-18).

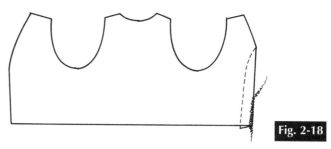

Fig. 2-18

A one-piece pattern makes this vest a cinch to serge. Embellish the front with flatlocked stems and flower buttons or as your imagination desires. Flat construction makes the serging fast and easy.

MATERIALS

1/2 yard for sizes 8–10 and 5/8 yard for sizes 12–14 of light- to medium-weight woven fabric for vest
Lining fabric, same yardages as above
One sheet of green craft foam (similar to felt, but more durable and washable)
Six large flower-shaped buttons
Two cones of decorative serger thread, such as pearl cotton, Pearl Crown Rayon, or woolly nylon
Three cones serger thread

Serger Set-Up

Stems: Wide, 3-thread, satin-length, flatlock stitch, decorative thread in upper looper, serger thread in needle and lower looper.

Edge finishing: Wide, 3-thread, satin-length, balanced stitch, decorative thread in loopers, serger thread in needle. Seaming: Wide, 3-thread, medium-length, balanced stitch, serger thread in loopers and needle.

Instructions

1 Enlarge pattern number 2 on copy machine. Cut one each of vest and lining fabric. Transfer lines for flower stems onto vest front with water soluble or disappearing marker.

2 Serge stems as follows: Fold vest front wrong sides together along stem marking. Serging

Bury tail chain at upper edges and use seam sealant at lower edge.

3 With wrong sides together, match all raw edges of vest and lining pieces. Decoratively serge-finish armholes and front and lower edges, leaving shoulder edges unserged (Fig. 2-19). Bury tail chains.

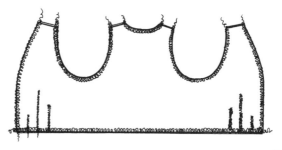

Fig. 2-19

4 Serge-seam shoulders, right sides together. Bury tail chains.

5 Cut small, free-hand leaves from craft foam and glue in place next to stems. Stitch a large flower button to upper tip of each stem (Fig. 2-20).

Fig. 2-20

Quick Tote

Fig. 2-21

Kids can never have enough totes in which to carry all of their stuff. This one features specially designed handles, with comfort grips, to make carrying that heavy load just a bit easier. Serge one to use as a library tote, doll carrier, or art bag, or even make one for yourself!

MATERIALS

1/2 yard of heavy canvas
8″ square of contrasting fabric for pocket
1/4 yard of poplin fabric for straps
12″ of 1/2″-diameter clear plastic tubing (available at hardware stores)
Three cones of woolly nylon or serger thread

Serger Set-Up

Medium, 3-thread, satin-length, balanced stitch, woolly nylon or serger thread in loopers and needle.

Instructions

1 Cut a 16″ × 27″ rectangle for tote body from canvas. Cut two 3″ × 39″ straps from poplin.

2 Serge-finish pocket upper and lower edges and tote body short edges. Interface pocket for extra stability if desired. Fold each strap in half lengthwise, wrong sides together. Serge-finish the long edges of each strap (Fig. 2-22).

3 Fold 1 1/2″ of finished edges to tote right side. Press, then topstitch close to serged edge.

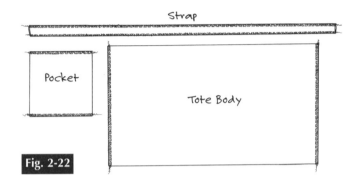

Fig. 2-22

4 Place pocket on tote right side, 4″ from upper and side edges. Top-stitch close to lower and side edges (Fig. 2-23).

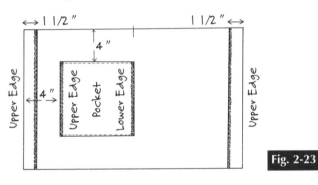

Fig. 2-23

5 Thread a 6″ piece of tubing into each handle piece, manipulating it to the strap center. Starting at lower edge of pocket, place straps along each pocket edge, continuing straight up, forming handles. Topstitch close to each serged edge, to tote's upper edges (Fig. 2-24).

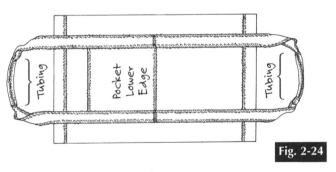

Fig. 2-24

6 Fold tote in half, right sides together, matching upper edges. Stitch a 5/8″ seam, then serge-finish. Bury tail chains, and turn right side out.

Ladies' Finery

Soft-Folds Belt

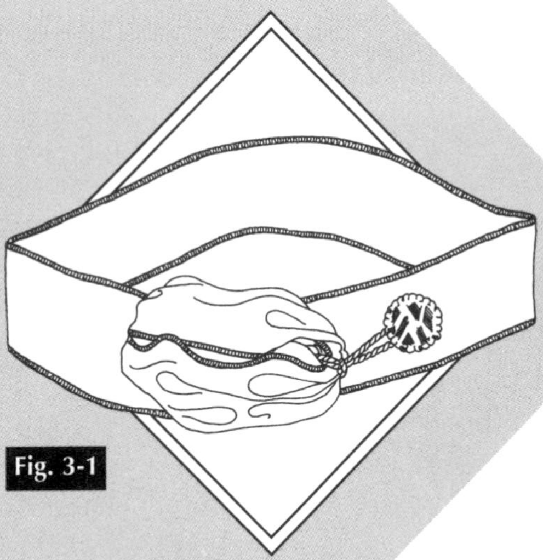

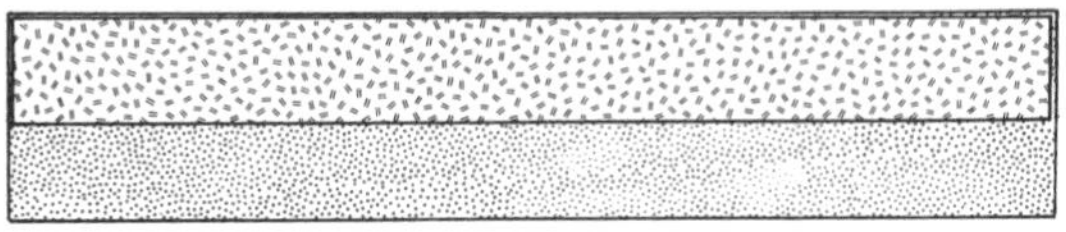

Fig. 3-2

3 Fold belt in half lengthwise, wrong sides together, sandwiching fleece between layers. Fuse.

4 Serge long edges of belt. Trim 3/4″ from one end for a loop. Serge short edges of belt and long edges of loop (Fig. 3-3).

Fig. 3-1

This easy-to-make belt looks great created from a variety of fabrics. Combine textures and surface treatments for an interesting and must-have fashion accessory. A distinctive button and a stretchy cord loop keep the soft folds in place.

MATERIALS

1/4 yard of light- to medium-weight woven fabric for belt
9″ × 18″ rectangle of soft, drapable contrast fabric for fold-back
1/4 yard of fleece
3/8 yard of fusible adhesive, such as HeatNBond Lite
6″ of stretch, elastic-type cord
One cone of decorative thread, such as woolly nylon metallic, Sulky Rayon, or Supertwist
Two cones of serger thread
One large, decorative shank-type button

Serger Set-Up

Medium, 3-thread, satin-length, wrapped stitch, decorative thread in upper looper, serger thread in lower looper and needle.

Instructions

1 Take exact waist measurement and cut a 5″-wide strip of belt fabric this length. Cut a 2 1/2″ wide fleece strip the same length. Cut 5″-wide strips of fusible adhesive this length, piecing as necessary to cover belt surface.

2 Fuse adhesive to wrong side of belt. Fuse fleece to half of belt lengthwise (Fig. 3-2).

Fig. 3-3

5 Topstitch loop onto one end of belt, right side, stitching close to narrow ends, forming a belt loop.

6 Serge-finish fold-back rectangle. Fold rectangle in half lengthwise, wrong sides together. Bring short ends together, butting sides. Gather through both ends in one continuous line of stitching (Fig. 3-4a).

7 Pin gathered fold-back to wrong side of opposite end of belt. Topstitch close to gathered serge-finished edges, catching in belt end (Fig. 3-4b).

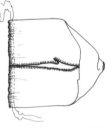

Fig. 3-4a

Fig. 3-4b

8 Knot elastic cord ends together and dot with seam sealant. Place cord through open loop end of contrast fold-back, and back through cord loop, slip-knot fashion.

9 Slide gathered loop under belt loop at opposite end, fold loop back over belt loop. Mark placement of button for loop closure, adjusting as necessary for fit. Stitch button in place. Loop cord over button to fasten.

Broomstick Skirt

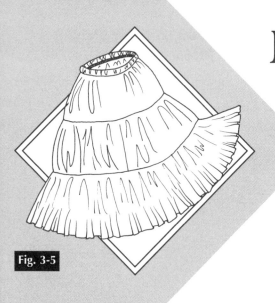

Fig. 3-5

The name of this wonderfully full and flattering skirt is derived from the method used to wrinkle the fabric. Years ago, to achieve wrinkles, a wet skirt was tied to a broomstick, and then left to dry for several days. Today you can serge a super quick version of this time-honored favorite and toss it in the dryer to set the wrinkles.

MATERIALS

2 1/3 yards of 60"-wide, lightweight cotton print fabric *or* 3 2/3 yards 45"-wide fabric
1 yard of 3/4"-wide nonroll elastic
6 yards of 3/8"-wide clear elastic
Three to four cones of serger thread
One pair of old pantyhose, one leg cut off and toe removed
Three large rubber bands

Serger Set-Up

Wide, 3- or 4-thread, medium-length, balanced stitch, serger thread in loopers and needles.

Instructions

1 Cut tiers as follows to determine tier widths: Figure finished skirt length (usually between 30"–33"), divide by three, then add 1" for seam allowances, casing, and hem. Use chart below for cutting tiers.

2 Right sides together, serge-seam tier pieces end to end, forming upper, middle, and lower tiers. Press seams in same direction (Fig. 3-6).

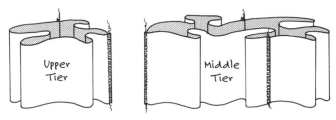

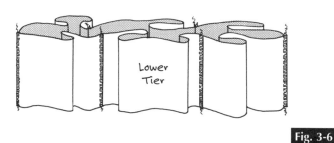

Fig. 3-6

3 To gather tiers, cut clear elastic the measurement of the bottom edge of upper tier. Stretch elastic before cutting. Quarter-mark elastic and top edge of middle tier. Matching markings, serge elastic to middle tier edge, stretching elastic to fit and forming even gathers. Repeat above sequence for lower tier (Fig. 3-7).

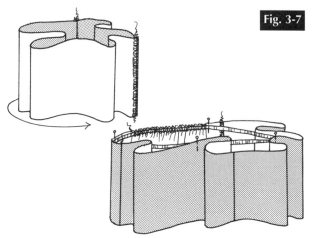

Fig. 3-7

	45" fabric	*60" fabric*
Upper tier	1 1/2 widths	1 width
Middle tier	3 widths	2 widths
Lower tier	6 widths	4 widths

4 Quarter-mark bottom edge of upper tier. With right sides together and matching quarter-markings on gathered top edge of middle tier, serge-seam upper and middle tiers. In same manner, serge-seam lower tier to middle tier.

5 Serge-finish top edge of skirt, then turn under 1″ to wrong side, forming casing. Measure elastic to fit, insert in casing, secure ends, and stitch opening closed. Serge-finish bottom edge of skirt with a rolled hem, or serge-finish, and turn under 1/4″ and topstitch.

6 To set wrinkles, wash skirt. Pull wet skirt through cut-off pantyhose leg, adjusting folds and gathers neatly. Secure pantyhose to skirt with rubber bands as shown. Place skirt in dryer and dry with several loads of laundry until completely dry (takes several hours). Remove pantyhose, wear, and enjoy. (Repeat drying procedure with each laundering to maintain wrinkling.) (Fig. 3-8).

Fig. 3-8

Yo-Yo Vest Cincher

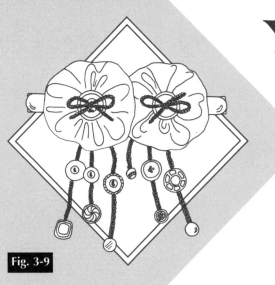

Fig. 3-9

This neat little cincher can be used to nip in the back of a vest, dress, or top. Serger yo-yos, along with antique buttons from grandma's cherished button box, make great decorative embellishments.

MATERIALS

1/4 yard of lightweight print or denim fabric
5" of 1"-wide elastic
Two suspender/vest clips
Assorted buttons
Fabric glue, such as Fabri Tac
Two cones of decorative thread, such as Jeans Stitch, pearl cotton, or Pearl Crown Rayon
Three cones of serger thread

Serger Set-Up

Serge-finishing: Narrow, 3-thread, medium-length, balanced stitch, serger thread in loopers and needle.

Seaming: Narrow, 3-thread, medium-length stitch, serger thread in loopers and needle.

Decorative chain cord: Narrow, 3-thread, satin-length, rolled-edge stitch, decorative thread in loopers, serger thread in needle.

Instructions

1 From the fabric, cut two circles for yo-yos using pattern number 3. Also cut a 2 3/4" × 8" strip for cincher casing.

2 Fold fabric strip in half lengthwise, wrong sides together. Flatlock-seam, then pull open gently. Pull elastic through casing, centering seam. Set machine for serge finishing. Serge-seam ends to secure (Fig. 3-10).

Fig. 3-10

3 Place ends of cincher through clip openings, fold over 1/2", then stitch to secure.

4 Serge-finish circles, serging over a filler cord (approximately 18" length of decorative thread), meeting but not overlapping stitches and taking care not to catch cord in serging. Gather yo-yo circles by pulling on ends of filler cord until gathers are as tight as possible. Tie into double knot. Dot knot with seam sealant and chain ends before trimming. Repeat with remaining circle (Fig. 3-11).

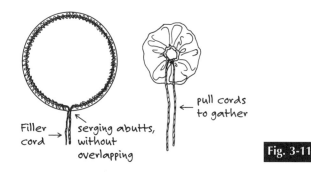

Filler cord → serging abutts, without overlapping

pull cords to gather ←

Fig. 3-11

5 Chain off approximately 1 yard of decorative cord. Cut chain into 10"–12" lengths. Thread cord through flatlock stitches on cincher, then thread buttons onto cord and tie buttons to ends (Fig. 3-12).

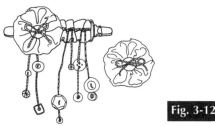

Fig. 3-12

6 Thread a small amount of cord through two flat buttons and tie into bows. Glue buttons on yo-yos to hide gathered edges. Glue yo-yos onto elasticized fabric cincher, covering flat-locking and ends of decorative cord.

Fig. 3-13

Sunburst Bead-Trimmed T-shirt

in radius, each 6″ long. These are the sunburst flatlock stitching lines (Fig. 3-14).

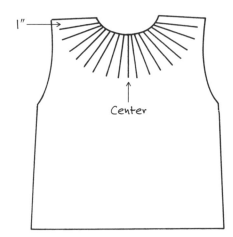

Fig. 3-14

This great-looking T-shirt is embellished with decorative flatlocking and tail chains left free. Beads are fastened onto the chains for a swingy necklace effect. Choose your own beads and color combination for a T-shirt that's sure to become a favorite in your wardrobe.

MATERIALS

Ribbed-neckline T-shirt, cut from favorite pattern
Five to seven different styles of beads, seventeen of each style
One cone of decorative thread, such as Pearl Crown Rayon, Designer 6, Decor 6, or Jeans Stitch
One spool of Sulky polyester monofilament thread
Three to four cones of serger thread

Serger Set-Up

Sunburst rows: Wide, 3-thread flatlock, satin-length stitch, decorative thread in upper looper, polyester monofilament in lower looper, serger thread in needle.

Seaming: Wide, 3/4 thread, medium-length, balanced stitch, serger thread in loopers and needle(s).

Instructions

1 On T-shirt front, mark neckline center, then 1″ from raw edge of shoulders. Divide and mark each of these sections in half, then in half, then in half again. Extend each marking 6″ from raw edge. You should have a total of seventeen lines

2 To create flatlocked sunburst, fold shirt wrong sides together along first marking line. Flatlock from neckline down, allowing serger stitches to hang halfway off the folded edge, following marking. Stop at end of mark, clear stitch finger, then chain for about 6″–8″. Repeat for remaining markings (Fig. 3-15).

Fig. 3-15

3 Pull flatlocking open gently and smooth out tail chains. Press lightly if desired. Slide beads

onto each 6″–8″ chain end, using a beading needle or wire needle/looper threader. Secure beads with an overhand knot dotted with seam sealant. Let dry, then trim chain (Fig. 3-16).

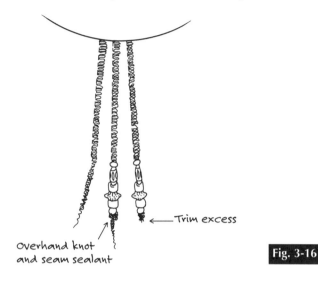

Overhand knot and seam sealant

Trim excess

Fig. 3-16

4 Construct balance of T-shirt using flat T-shirt construction: Serge one shoulder seam, apply neckline ribbing, serge remaining shoulder seam, decoratively flatlock hems on sleeves, serge sleeves to armholes, and serge underarm/side seams. Finally, serge-finish hem, then turn up and topstitch.

NOTE: For proper care, be sure to check bead package for washability. To machine wash T-shirt, turn inside out and place inside of a lingerie or hosiery bag. Wash in cold water on gentle cycle, or hand wash. Let drip dry, press lightly if needed.

Accessories Holder

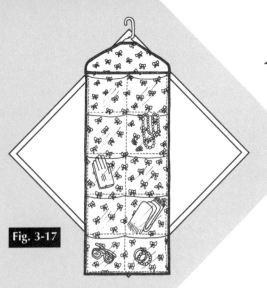

Stash all of your accessories in these big, clear vinyl pockets. Easy to serge and a great organizer for anything from hosiery to sunglasses. This space-saving holder can be displayed on a door or hung inside a closet.

MATERIALS

1 yard of 54″-wide decorator fabric
1/2 yard of 8-gauge vinyl
1/2 yard of tear-away fabric stabilizer such as Tear-Easy, cut into 1″ strips
1 1/2 yards of heavyweight fusible interfacing, such as Craft Fuse
Two cones of decorative thread, such as pearl cotton, Designer 6, Decor 6, or Pearl Crown Rayon
One cone of serger thread
Plastic tubular hanger

Serger Set-Up

Wide, 3-thread, satin-length, balanced stitch, decorative thread in loopers, serger thread in needle.

Instructions

1 From decorator fabric, cut one 18″ × 54″ rectangle, and one 9″ × 18″ rectangle. From vinyl, cut five 9″ × 17 1/2″ pockets.

> Cut vinyl on gridded cutting board, masking off area on board to be used as cutting template.

2 Fuse interfacing to wrong side of both fabric rectangles. Cut hanger pocket from small rectangle using pattern #4. Place hanger pocket crosswise on right side of holder back piece, matching raw upper edges, then trim away excess fabric to match hanger pocket edges.

3 Serge-finish the upper and lower edges of hanger pocket and holder back piece (Fig. 3-18).

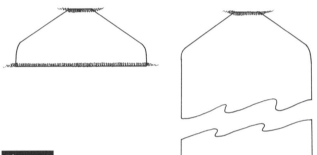

Fig. 3-18

4 Right sides up and raw edges matching, place hanger pocket on holder back. Serge-finish both long sides of holder/hanger pocket (Fig. 3-19). Bury tail chains.

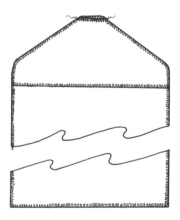

Fig. 3-19

5 Lay clear vinyl pockets on holder right side, leaving a scant 1/8″ between each. Pin each pocket close to edge in two places to prevent shifting. Edge stitch lower edge of each pocket, stitching over fabric stabilizer strips. Stitch each pocket side edge, backstitching at upper edge of each to reinforce. Mark center of each pocket with masking tape, then stitch down center, over tear-away strips, backstitching for reinforcement at upper edge of each pocket. Remove masking tape and tear-away stabilizer (Fig. 3-20).

6 Insert tubular hanger into hanger pocket and hang the accessories holder in closet or on hook.

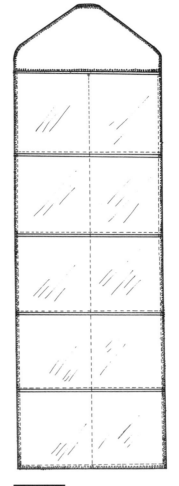

Fig. 3-20

Ponytail Scarf

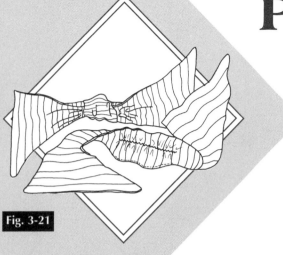

Fig. 3-21

Because of the elastic inside and its the special shape, this scarf won't slip out of a ponytail. Serge them up in a flash; just choose a fabric that drapes well.

MATERIALS

1/4 yard of lightweight fabric
3 1/2" of 1/4"-wide elastic
Three to four cones of serger thread

Serger Set-Up

Medium, 3/4-thread, medium-length, balanced stitch, serger thread in loopers and needle(s).

Instructions

1 Connect pattern number 5A to 5B. Cut two scarf pieces from fabric using complete pattern.

2 On wrong side of one scarf piece, mark center, then mark 2 1/2" from each side of center mark. Zigzag elastic to center of scarf, stretching elastic to match markings (Fig. 3-22).

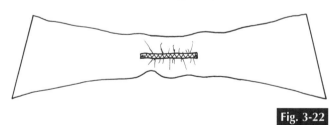

Fig. 3-22

3 Place both scarf pieces right sides together with raw edges matching, and serge-seam scarves together, leaving a small opening at one edge for turning (Fig. 3-23). Turn scarf right side out, then stitch opening closed, close to edge.

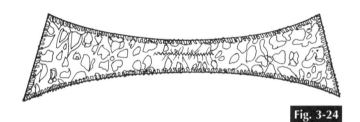

Fig. 3-23

TIP For a different look, after step 2, place pieces wrong sides together, and finish all edges with a narrow decorative stitch (Fig. 3-24).

Fig. 3-24

To keep scarf from slipping in even the finest hair, instead of zigzagging elastic to wrong side of piece, use clear elastic and zigzag to right side of piece. The elastic will gently and inconspicuously grip the hair when scarf is tied.

Guy Stuff

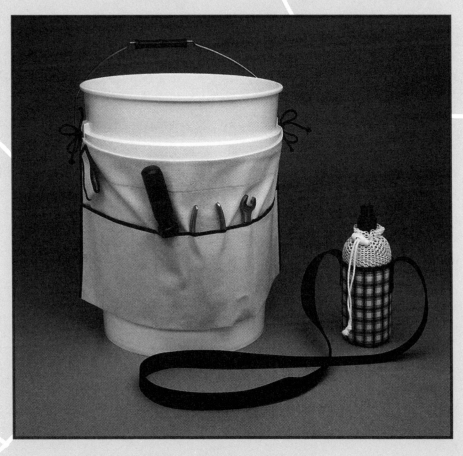

Corner Bookmark

Fig. 4-1

Mark a book's page in style with this neat bookmark. Serge in a masculine print or a suedelike fabric, then finish with decorative thread. Monogram it for a personalized touch. It makes a great gift, especially when given with a special book.

MATERIALS

Two rectangles of fabric, at least 5″ × 8″
One 5″ × 8″ rectangle of HeatNBond Lite
One cone of decorative thread, such as woolly
    nylon, Supertwist, or Sulky Rayon
Two cones of serger thread

Serger Set-Up

Narrow, 3-thread, satin-length, balanced stitch, decorative thread in upper looper, serger thread in lower looper and needle.

Instructions

1 Fuse HeatNBond to wrong side of one fabric rectangle. Fuse this to other fabric rectangle, wrong sides together, creating a reversible rectangle piece (Fig. 4-2).

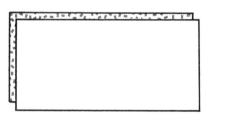

Fig. 4-2

2 Using pattern number 6, cut one bookmark from fused fabric. Serge-finish two short edges and one long edge (Fig. 4-3).

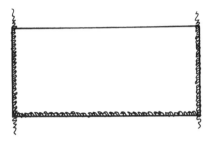

Fig. 4-3

3 Fold rectangle in half crosswise, matching raw edges. With right sides together, serge-seam (Fig. 4-4a). Press seam to one side. Turn bookmark right side out, centering seam at back as shown. Press to set creases in bookmark (Fig. 4-4b).

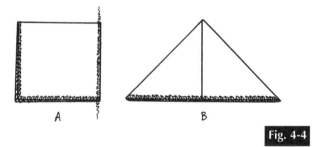

A   B

Fig. 4-4

This is a perfect small project for experimenting with a variety of embellishments. Before constructing the bookmark, monogram center of right side of bookmark piece. Try stitching several rows of decorative machine stitching on the diagonal, using tone-on-tone coloration. Couch serger chain to surface in a random or stripe pattern. The possibilities are endless.

Water Bottle Tote

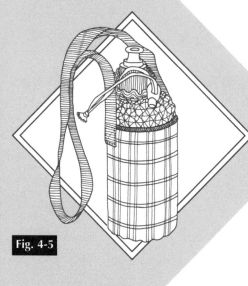

Fig. 4-5

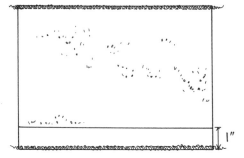

Fig. 4-6

Here's an easy way to carry a bottle of water. Place bottle in terry-lined holder and pull drawstring to secure. Its soft shape fits a variety of water bottle sizes. Guys and gals alike will want one of these, so get ready to serge several.

MATERIALS

One 7″ × 10 1/2″ rectangle of light- to medium-weight fabric
One 6″ × 10 1/2″ rectangle of terry
One 6″ × 10 1/2″ rectangle of mesh fabric
One 6″ × 10 1/2″ rectangle of HeatNBond Lite
1 1/2 yards of 1″-wide webbing for strap (optional)
3/4 yard of 1/8″ polyester cord for drawstring
12″ of 1/4″ elastic
One cord lock
Three cones of woolly nylon or serger thread

Serger Set-Up

Medium, 3-thread, satin-length, balanced stitch, woolly nylon or serger thread in loopers and needle.

Instructions

1 Fuse HeatNBond to wrong side of light- to medium-weight fabric rectangle, matching upper and side edges (lower 1″ of fabric will not be fused). Wrong sides together and matching raw edges, fuse terry to fabric piece (Fig. 4-6).

2 Serge-finish upper and lower edge of fabric/terry piece. Fold mesh in half lengthwise. Lap upper finished edge of fabric/terry piece 1/2″ over mesh raw edges. Topstitch close to serged

edge. Turn under 1″ casing at lower edge. Top-stitch close to serged edge, stopping 1″ from each end (Fig. 4-7).

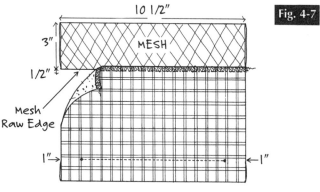

Fig. 4-7

3 Right sides together, serge side seam. Insert elastic into casing, gather bottom tight, and tie elastic into double knot. Trim elastic ends close to knot and tuck under casing. Thread cord through holes in upper edge of mesh. Slide cord lock onto both ends of drawstring, knot ends together, then trim away excess cord (Fig. 4-8).

Fig. 4-8

4 For an optional carry strap, trim ends of webbing, and heat seal or use seam sealant to keep ends from raveling. Mark one side of carrier, place raw edge of strap 1″ below finished fabric edge, and topstitch in square shape for extra security. Repeat for other side.

Tool Tote Apron

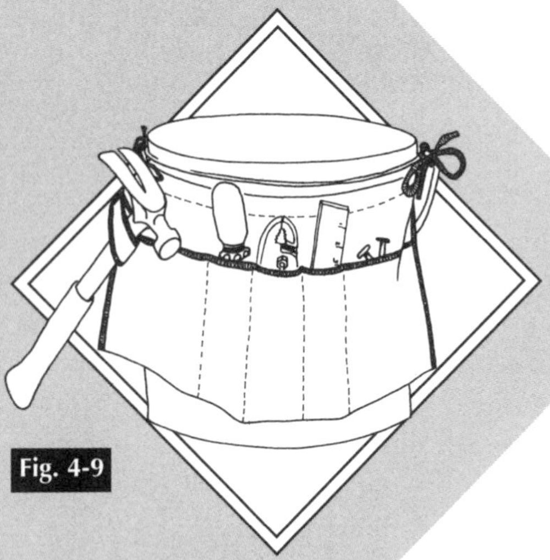

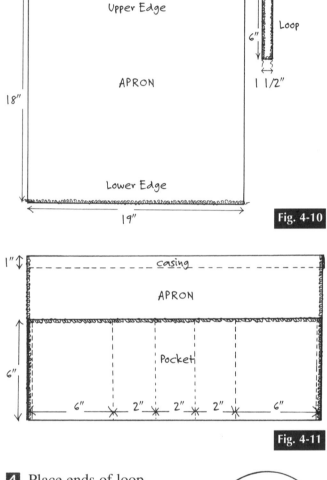

Fig. 4-9

Your favorite guy will appreciate this handy tool tote apron. Tied to a five-gallon bucket (look at local bakeries for throwaways), this tool organizer can hold anything from screwdrivers and hammers to nuts and bolts. Large items fit in the bucket for convenient carrying to and from all those "honey-do" jobs.

MATERIALS

1/2 yard of canvas or denim
1 yard of 1/8" polyester cord for ties
Three cones of woolly nylon or serger thread

Serger Set-Up

Medium, 3-thread, satin-length, balanced stitch, woolly nylon or serger thread in loopers and needle.

Instructions

1. From canvas, cut one 18" × 19" rectangle and one 3" × 6" rectangle for loop.

2. Serge-finish 19" (upper and lower) edges of large rectangle for apron. Fold small rectangle in half lengthwise, wrong sides together. Serge-finish all edges of small rectangle for loop (Fig. 4-10).

3. Fold up lower edge 6" to apron right side, forming pocket. Serge-seam sides, catching in pocket edges. At upper edge, turn under 1" to wrong side, and topstitch close to serged edge. Stitch pocket divisions as shown, backstitching at pocket upper edges for reinforcement (Fig. 4-11).

Fig. 4-10

Fig. 4-11

4. Place ends of loop together. On right side of tote pocket at one upper corner, place loop at an angle and topstitch close to ends (Fig. 4-12).

5. Cut cord in half, making two 18" pieces. Stitch cord close to upper corners, through center of cord, forming ties.

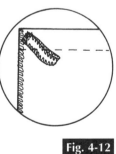

Fig. 4-12

Tie apron to handle of the five-gallon bucket. The hammer can be placed through the fabric loop and other tools can be stored in the pockets. Two aprons can be tied to a bucket, one on each side, for extra storage.

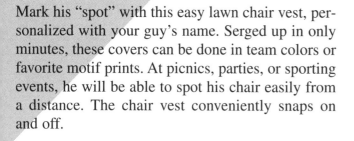

Fig. 4-13

Lawn Chair Vest

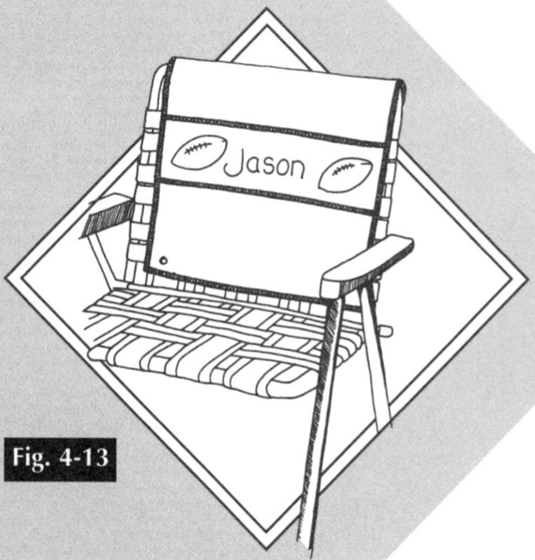

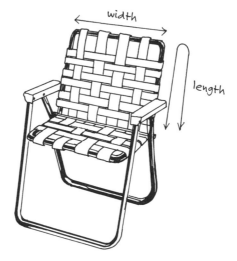

Fig. 4-14

Mark his "spot" with this easy lawn chair vest, personalized with your guy's name. Serged up in only minutes, these covers can be done in team colors or favorite motif prints. At picnics, parties, or sporting events, he will be able to spot his chair easily from a distance. The chair vest conveniently snaps on and off.

MATERIALS

1/2 yard of medium-weight poplin or denim
1/4 yard of contrast fabric for center strip
Two sets of decorative snaps
One cone of decorative thread, such as Jeans Stitch, woolly nylon, or Sulky Rayon
Two cones of serger thread
Fabric paint

Serger Set-Up

Medium, 3-thread, satin-length, balanced stitch, decorative thread in upper looper, serger thread in lower looper and needle.

Instructions

1 For chair vest width, measure across upper back edge of lawn chair. For chair vest length, measure from seat and up over back to back lower edge. Cut fabric this width and length for vest (Fig. 4-14).

2 Cut a 7″ strip of contrast fabric the same width as chair vest (see step 1 above). Serge-finish both long sides of contrast strip. Fold vest in half crosswise, marking center fold. On front half of vest, place contrast piece halfway between fold and lower edge. Topstitch contrast piece to vest front close to serged edges (Fig. 4-15).

3 Serge-finish short edges of vest, right side facing up. Serge-finish long edges, catching in contrast piece. Bury tail chains. Place decorative snaps at each corner (Fig. 4-16).

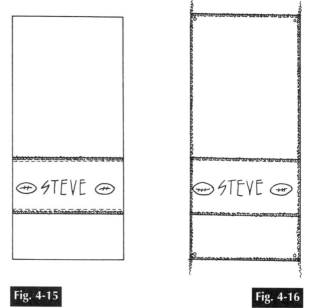

Fig. 4-15

Fig. 4-16

Eyeglasses Case

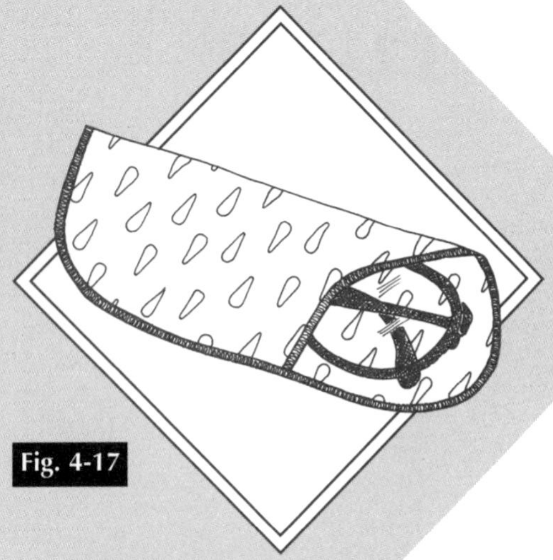

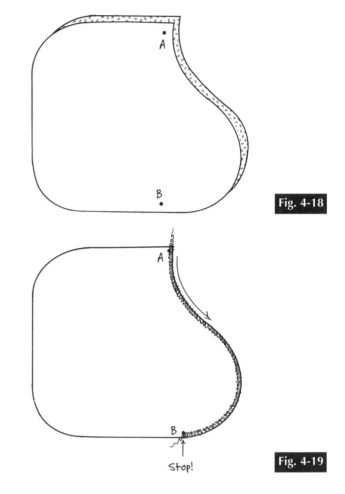

Fig. 4-17

Keep sunglasses or reading glasses safe and in their place with this quick-serged eyeglasses case. The one-piece design makes serging super simple. Fused padding gives just the right amount of loftiness to protect lenses.

MATERIALS

One 8″ × 18″ rectangle of lightweight cotton print
    (avoid polyester—it tends to scratch plastic lenses)
One 8″ × 9″ rectangle of polyester fleece
One 8″ × 18″ rectangle of HeatNBond Lite
Three cones of woolly nylon, Sulky Rayon, or serger
    thread

Serger Set-Up

Medium, 3-thread, satin-length, balanced stitch, woolly nylon, Sulky Rayon, or serger thread in loopers and needle.

Instructions

1 Fuse HeatNBond to wrong side of fabric rectangle. Place fleece on wrong side of one half of fabric piece. Fuse in place. Fold fabric over fleece and fuse, sandwiching fleece between both layers of fabric. Using pattern number 7, cut one eyeglasses case from padded fabric, transferring markings (Fig. 4-18).

2 Serge-finish top edge of case from point "A" to point "B." Do not remove case from serger (Fig. 4-19).

Fig. 4-18

Fig. 4-19

3 Lift serger presser foot. Carefully fold case in half, matching "A" with "B." Continue serging remaining edges, catching in both layers. Bury tail chains (Fig. 4-20).

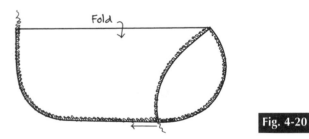

Fig. 4-20

4 To reinforce opening, topstitch for approximately 1/2″ close to serged edge at crossover (where "A" meets "B"), backstitching two to three times.

TOP: *Easy-Fit Head Band and Sneaker Peekers (Chapter 2).* This polar fleece headband is just right for keeping ears toasty on frigid days. Sneaker Peekers and serged laces help dress up plain sneakers.

MIDDLE: *Yo-Yo Vest Cincher and Soft-Folds Belt (Chapter 3).* This Yo-Yo Vest Cincher looks equally great cinching in the back of a dress, vest, or top. The Soft-Folds Belt combines fabric textures and metallic thread for an elegant accessory.

LEFT: *Pocket Blanket (Chapter 6).* This polar fleece Pocket Blanket forms a pillow when folded into its own attached pocket.

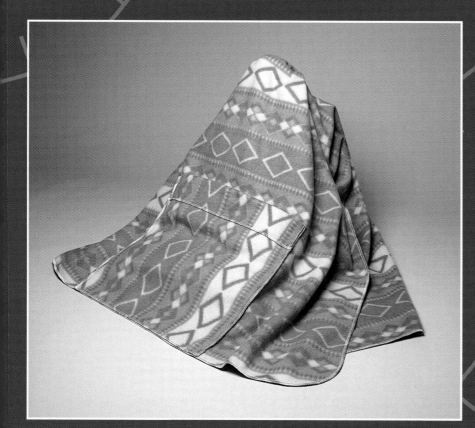

Mantel Scarf (Chapter 6). Dress up and protect your fireplace mantel with a decorative scarf. This one is embellished with buttons on the ends for hanging charms and ornaments.

Christmas Stocking, Elegant Serged Ornaments, and Serged Cards and Tags (Chapter 9). Holiday decorating, serger style, will make for memorable festive decor.

Fifteen-Minute Gift Bags and Heirloom Bread Basket Liner (Chapter 8). These gift bags make wrapping a present (especially cookies) a snap! The Heirloom Bread Basket Liner is a pretty addition to any table setting.

Wall Pocket and TV Guide *Cover/Remote Holder (Chapter 5).* Use this Wall Pocket for storing and stowing lightweight toys, magazines, and other clutter. Put an end to the lost remote with this handy *TV Guide* Cover and Remote Holder.

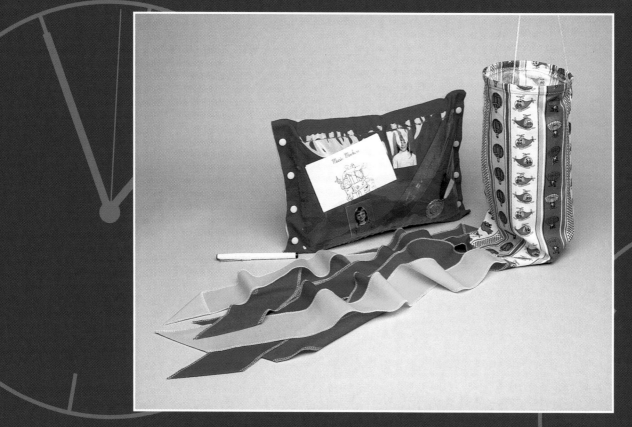

Keepsake Autograph Pillow and Serger Windsock (Chapter 7). Kids will love to show off awards and friends' signatures with this Keepsake Autograph Pillow. The Serger Windsock can blow outside in the breeze or hang inside for cute kids' decor.

Quilt-Block Banner (Chapter 7). Hang this flatlocked Quilt-Block Banner on a wall or outside on a flag/banner pole.

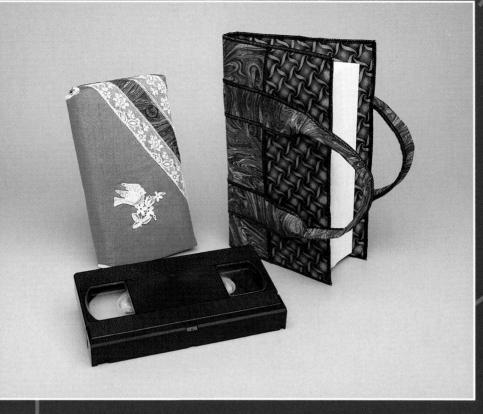

Video Box Cover and Book/Bible Cover (Chapter 8). Make a special video "album" with this serged Video Box Cover. A handy, padded cover makes take-along reading convenient.

Easter Gift Basket and All-Occasion Candle Rings (Chapter 9). Spring flowers look especially cheery in this Easter Gift Basket. The All-Occasion Candle Rings add a lovely touch to plain tapers.

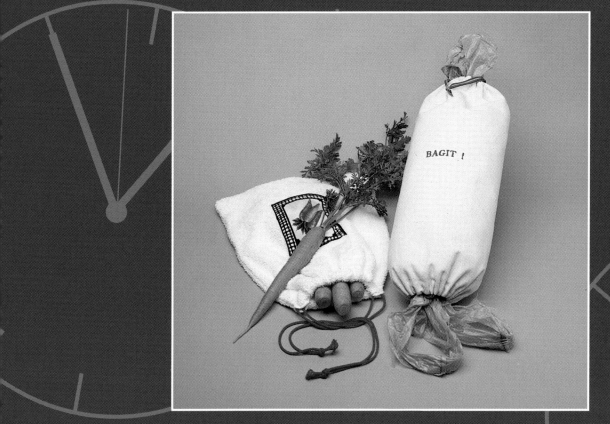

Terry Crisper Bag and Bag It! Bags (Chapter 5). Store washed veggies in this dampened Terry Crisper Bag, for fresh keeping. Store plastic grocery bags for easy dispensing in the Bag It! bag.

Tool Tote Apron and Water Bottle Tote (Chapter 4). Your favorite guy will appreciate this take-anywhere bucket with attached Tool Tote Apron. The Water Bottle Tote keeps drinks cool and hands dry.

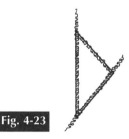

Fig. 4-21

Five Triangles Appliquéd Sweatshirt

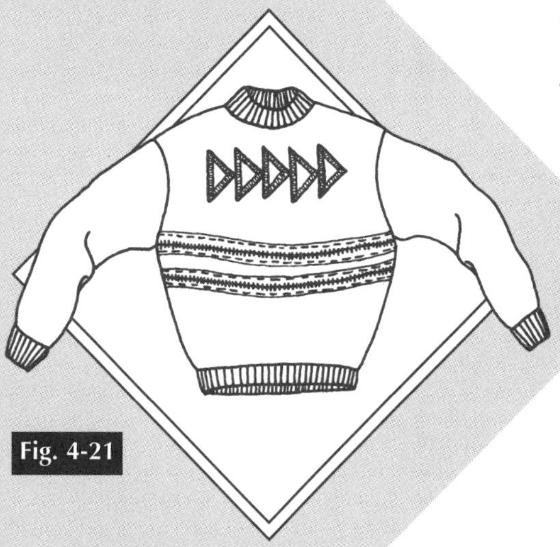

Five appliquéd triangles, along with some flatlocked rugby stripes, transform a plain sweatshirt from ho-hum to downright handsome in a matter of minutes. Scraps of masculine print and textured fabrics are used to create these easy-to-serge appliqués.

MATERIALS

Solid color crewneck sweatshirt
1/4 yard of print fabric
Three 4″ squares of different print or textured fabrics
1/4 yard of HeatNBond Lite
Three cones of woolly nylon, Sulky Rayon, or serger thread

Serger Set-Up

Serge-finished edges: Narrow, 3-thread, satin-length, balanced stitch, woolly nylon, Sulky Rayon, or serger thread in loopers and needle.

Flatlock: Medium, 3-thread flatlock, medium-length stitch, woolly nylon, Sulky Rayon, or serger thread in loopers and needle.

Instructions

1 From print fabric, cut two 3 1/2″-wide strips the length of the fabric width. Fold each strip in half lengthwise, right sides together. Flatlock the long raw edges (Fig. 4-22).

Fig. 4-22

2 Pull serging flat, turn tubes right side out (a FASTURN tube turner makes easy work of this), and press with flatlocking centered on tube.

3 Fuse HeatNBond to wrong side of 4″ fabric squares. Cut each square in half diagonally, forming two triangles from each. Serge-finish all sides of five of the triangles (discard the sixth one). Bury tail chains (Fig. 4-23).

Fig. 4-23

4 Place one tube, flatlocked side up, on sweatshirt front, under sleeves and across chest area. Trim tube to fit shirt front. Topstitch close to each folded edge, turning under raw ends. Stitch second tube 1 1/2″ below first one (Fig. 4-24).

1 1/2″

Fig. 4-24

5 Center first (odd) triangle on sweatshirt, then place others (pairs, with one on each side of center triangle), points touching, as illustrated. Space all triangles evenly between neckline and edge of first stripe. Fuse triangles in place, then topstitch around each close to serge-finished edge.

CHAPTER

5

Nifty Storage and Handy Helpers

Bag It!

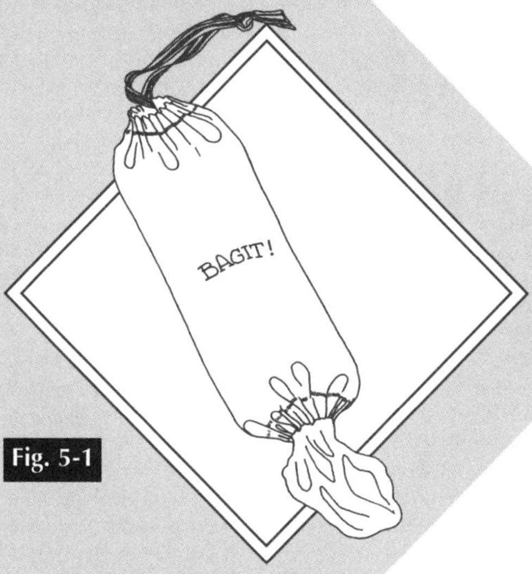

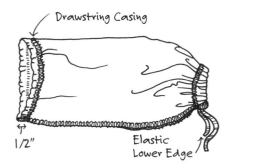

Fig. 5-1

Serge this handy bag with top and bottom openings to hold and dispense all those plastic grocery bags neatly and conveniently. Anyone who sees this ingenious little organizer will be requesting one for themselves, so make several!

MATERIALS

1/2 yard of medium-weight cotton poplin fabric
   (makes two bags)
6" of 3/8"-wide braided elastic
1/2 yard of cord or ribbon for top drawstring
Three cones of serger thread
Embroidery thread or fabric paint (optional)

Serger Set-Up

Seaming and edge finishing: Wide width, 3-thread, medium-length, balanced stitch, serger thread through needle and loopers.

Flatlocked hems: Wide, 3-thread flatlock, medium-length stitch, loosening needle tension to form flatlock stitch, serger thread through needle and loopers.

Instructions

1 Cut poplin to 20" × 18" (18" edges are top and bottom, 20" edges are sides). Optional: Embroider or fabric paint BAGIT! in the center. Serge-finish each 20" edge (Fig. 5-2).

2 To make casing, press under 1" hems on top and bottom. Make a flatlocked hem on each end, folding fabric so the ladder stitch is visible from the right side (Fig. 5-3).

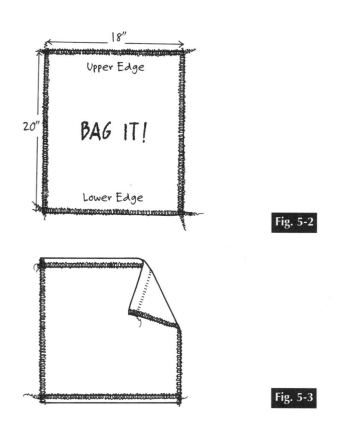

Fig. 5-2

Fig. 5-3

3 Fold bag in half, right sides together, matching serge-finished sides. Straight stitch a 3/8" seam, starting and stopping 1/2" from each hemmed end, reinforcing stitching at ends.

4 Insert elastic into bottom casing, lap ends 1/2", and stitch to secure (Fig. 5-4).

Fig. 5-4

5 Thread cord or ribbon into top casing and knot ends together. Turn bag right side out. Place plastic bags through drawstring opening (don't be afraid to stuff tight), and dispense through elastic opening at lower edge.

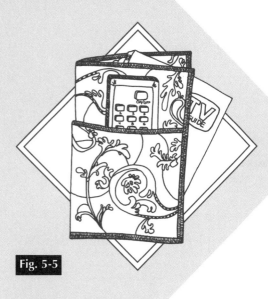

Fig. 5-5

TV Guide Cover and Remote Holder

Give your favorite couch potato this handy *TV Guide* cover. A storage pocket holds the remote. A layered fusing technique gives the cover just the right amount of stability and stiffness.

MATERIALS

3/4 yard of lightweight decorator fabric
3/4 yard of polyester fleece
1 yard of fusible adhesive, such as HeatNBond Lite
Three cones of woolly nylon

Serger Set-Up

Medium width, 3 thread satin-length, balanced stitch, woolly nylon in needle and loopers.

Instructions

1 Cut the following from both the decorator fabric and fusible adhesive: Two 12″ × 8 1/2″ rectangles, two 12″ × 5 1/2″ rectangles, and four 5″ × 8 1/2″ rectangles. From the polyester fleece, cut one 12″ × 8 1/2″ rectangle and one 12″ × 5 1/2″ rectangle.

2 Press fusible adhesive to the wrong sides of 12″ × 8 1/2″ fabric rectangles, 12″ × 5 1/2″ rectangles, and two of the 5″ × 8 1/2″ rectangles. Fuse the remaining 5″ × 8 1/2″ fabric rectangles wrong sides together to make two flaps (without padding). Sandwich fleece between layers of the two large rectangles as shown to create double-sided padded rectangles (Fig. 5-6).

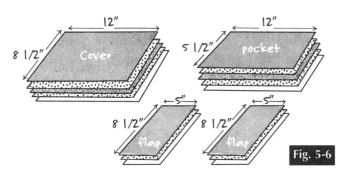

Fig. 5-6

3 Serge-finish one long edge on each inside flap and one long edge of pocket. Do not trim fabric edge while serging (Fig. 5-7).

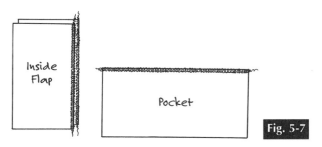

Fig. 5-7

4 Layer pieces as shown: Pocket, cover, then inside flaps. Use transparent tape instead of pins to keep layers from shifting while serging. Serge sides and upper and lower edges, catching in all layers (Fig. 5-8).

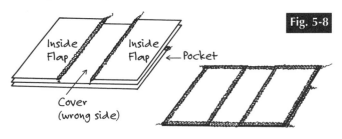

Fig. 5-8

5 Bury tail chains and slip *TV Guide* inside flaps and remote in pocket. Bring on the popcorn!

Write-on, Wipe-off Bulletin Board

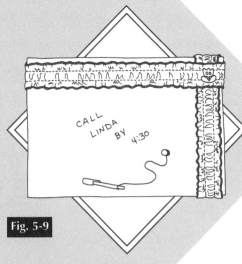

Fig. 5-9

Serged ruffle trim and laminated fabric turn an ordinary piece of craft foam board into a convenient write-on, wipe off bulletin board. Coordinate fabrics to match your kitchen or rec room decor, attach magnets or picture wire, and display for all the gang to see.

MATERIALS

3/4 yard of lightweight solid woven fabric (to be laminated)
1/4 yard of decorator print fabric
1/2 yard of HeatNBond Iron-on Vinyl, matte finish
1 1/2 yards of 1"-wide elastic
Foam core board, 18" × 24"
Three cones of woolly nylon
One package of wide bias tape
One small Velcro dot
Spray adhesive
Fabric glue or glue gun
Sticky-back magnets or picture wire

Serger Set-Up

Narrow, rolled-hem, satin-length stitch, woolly nylon in loopers and needle.

Instructions

1 Laminate a 24" × 30" piece of solid-colored fabric with Iron-On Vinyl following manufacturer's instructions.

2 Apply laminated fabric to foam core board using spray adhesive. Apply adhesive to face of one side of foam board and wrong side of

laminated piece for maximum adhesion. Place foam board in center of laminated fabric, sprayed sides together. Fold corners to wrong side and glue in place with fabric glue or glue gun. Fold and glue all raw edges to back; let dry (Fig. 5-10).

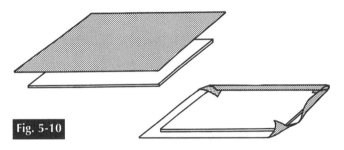

Fig. 5-10

3 Cut a 4" × 36" and a 4" × 45" strip of decorator fabric. Roll hem long edges of each. Cut a piece of bias tape to fit the length of each strip. Press bias edges open. Fold each fabric strip and bias pieces in half lengthwise; press mark center of each.

4 Place bias strip down center back of each fabric strip of the same length, matching center markings. Stitch 1/8" from each long side of bias edge. Cut a 30" piece and a 24" piece from elastic. Insert elastic through bias strip casings (24" piece through 36" strip, 30" piece through 45" strip), anchoring each end with machine stitching (Fig. 5-11). Stretch each finished strip to distribute fullness evenly along elastic.

Fig. 5-11

5 Glue ruffled trim to laminated foam board in crisscross fashion, folding raw ends to back side (Fig. 5-12). Chain off a 24″ length of thread chain to use as cord to hang marking pen. Tie cord around pen and glue loop Velcro dot over knot. Make a knot in end of serged chain, place under hook Velcro dot, then glue dot to face of finished board. Attach magnets or picture wire to finished board back for hanging.

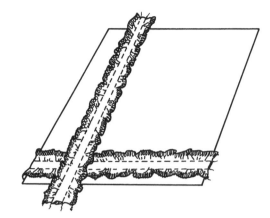

Fig. 5-12

Wall Pockets

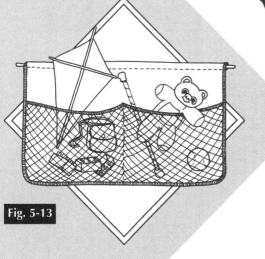

Fig. 5-13

These easy-to-make pockets give you instant storage anywhere. My daughter uses them to hold small dolls and stuffed animals in her bedroom, but they work equally well for lightweight bathroom essentials and bedside items.

MATERIALS

1/2 yard of light- to medium-weight woven print fabric
3/8 yard of mesh fabric
1 yard of heavyweight fusible interfacing
28″ of 1/4″-wide clear elastic
3/8″ dowel rod cut to 36″ long
Three cones of serger thread
Optional: Two cones of decorative serger thread

Serger Set-Up

Applying elastic and serge finishing upper edge: Narrow width, 3-thread, medium-length, balanced stitch, serger thread through loopers and needle.

Finishing outside edge of pocket: Medium to wide, 3-thread, short-length stitch, serger thread or decorative thread through loopers and matching thread through needle.

Instructions

1 From fabric and interfacing, cut an 18″ × 32″ rectangle for pocket back. From mesh, cut a 12″ × 32″ rectangle for pocket pouch. Fuse interfacing to wrong side of fabric. Round lower edges of fabric pocket back and mesh pouch by tracing around a dinner plate as a guide.

2 Serge clear elastic to inside upper (straight) edge of pouch, stretching elastic to fit while serging.

3 Serge-finish upper (straight) edge of pocket back (Fig. 5-14).

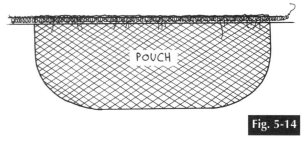

Fig. 5-14

4 Place mesh pouch on top of right side of pocket back, matching lower and side raw edges. Serge around outer edges, catching in both layers (Fig. 5-15).

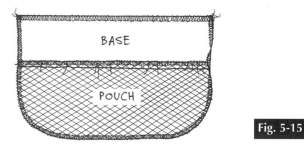

Fig. 5-15

5 Reinforce side edges of pocket with a 2″ line of stitching close to serger stitching. Stitch through center of pouch, reinforcing at upper edge, to divide into two. Fold under 1″ at base upper edge and stitch close to finished edge to form casing (Fig. 5-16).

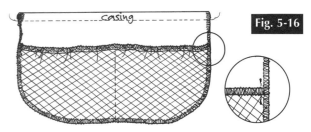

Fig. 5-16

6 Insert dowel rod through casing. Attach to wall using appropriate-size cup hooks. Slide dowel through center of hooks. Let the clean-up begin!

Terry Crisper Bag

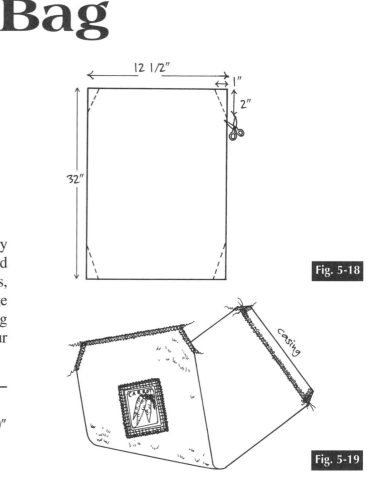

Fig. 5-17

Keep vegetables crisp and fresh with this handy terry drawstring bag. Just run cold water over the bag and wring out excess moisture, fill it with washed veggies, and pop it into the refrigerator. This easy-to-serge design is also great for making any kind of drawstring bag in a jiffy. Just modify the bag size to suit your needs.

Fig. 5-18

Fig. 5-19

MATERIALS

One bath-size terry towel, approximately 25″ × 40″
   or larger (makes two)
1 1/2 yards of cord for drawstring
Fabric appliqué (optional)
Three cones of woolly nylon

Serger Set-Up

Medium-width, 3-thread, medium-length, balanced stitch, woolly nylon in loopers and needle.

Instructions

1. Cut a 12 1/2″ × 32″ rectangle from terry bath towel (Fig. 5-18). Fold rectangle in half crosswise and trim off a 1″ × 2″ triangle from each upper corner.

2. Optional: Serge-finish edges of appliqué piece. Topstitch in place in center of one half of bag piece.

3. Serge-finish upper edges and corner angles. Fold under 1″ on both upper edges, and topstitch close to serge-finished edge to form casing (Fig. 5-19).

4. Fold bag in half crosswise with right sides together and raw edges matching. Serge side seams. Cut drawstring cord into two 27″ pieces. Thread each piece through a casing and knot ends together (Fig. 5-20).

5. Prepare bag and fill with veggies as described above. Pull drawstrings and tie into bow. Keep bag in refrigerator at least four hours or overnight for perfect veggie crispness.

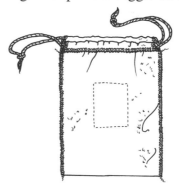

Fig. 5-20

CHAPTER

6

Hearth and Home

One-Hour Swag Valance

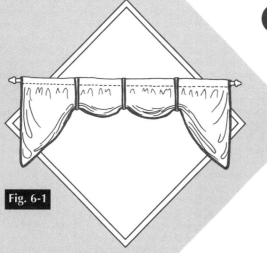

Fig. 6-1

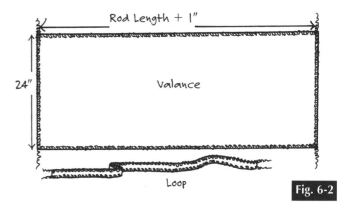

Fig. 6-2

Custom-make this pretty swag valance for any window. Choose a decorator fabric to match the room, then finish the edges with contrasting decorative thread for a piped-edge look.

MATERIALS

Decorator fabric for valance and tabs (measure rod end to end plus 1"; divide amount by 36" to figure yardage)

One cone of decorative thread, such as Supertwist, FS Jewel, Sulky Rayon, woolly nylon, or woolly nylon metallic

Two cones of serger thread

Standard or cafe rod

Serger Set-Up

Rolled-hem, satin-length stitch, decorative thread in upper looper and serger thread in lower looper and needle.

Instructions

1 Cut fabric for valance: Length—length of rod plus 1"; depth—24". Cut one 4" × 20" strip for each swag loop (you will need two or more loops to swag valance; the larger the window, the more loops you'll need).

2 Serge-finish valance with rolled edge. Press each loop in half lengthwise, wrong sides together. Roll-hem long edges of each loop. Dot corners with seam sealant, let dry, then trim (Fig. 6-2).

3 Turn under a 3 1/2" casing at valance upper edge. Topstitch close to serge-finished edge. Fold each swag loop in half crosswise, and serge-seam ends, forming a loop (Fig. 6-3).

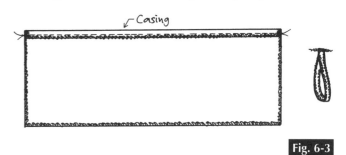

Fig. 6-3

4 Slide rod into valance casing, then place loops over rod and valance, positioning swag loops evenly and adjusting valance for draped swag effect. Hang rod as per manufacturer's instructions. Readjust swags after hanging if necessary (Fig. 6-4).

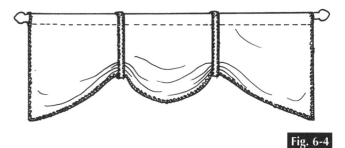

Fig. 6-4

Flatlocked Table Runner

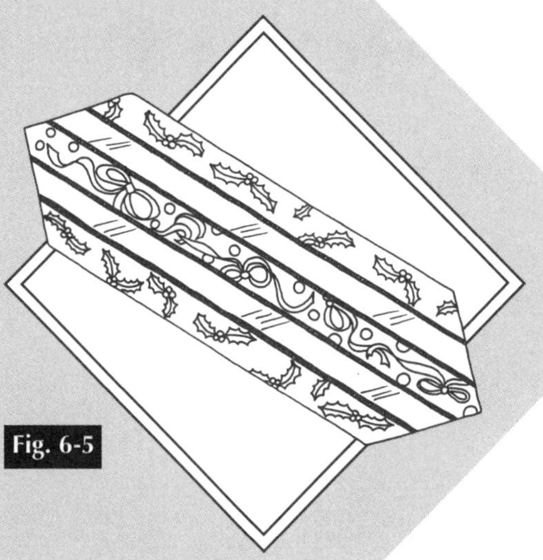

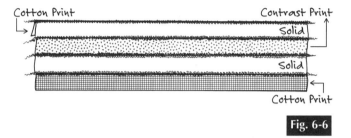

Fig. 6-5

Make a table runner by strip quilting, flatlock style. Decorative threads are shown at their best in this easy-to-serge project. Serge it fancy with lamé, gilded fabrics, and sparkling metallic threads. Or serge it simple with pretty cotton prints, solids, and pearl cotton or topstitching thread. Either way, this flatlocked table runner will be an attractive addition to your table setting.

MATERIALS

1/4 yard of 45"-wide lightweight cotton print fabric
1/4 yard of 45"-wide lightweight cotton solid or bonded lamé fabric
1/8 yard of 45"-wide contrasting, lightweight cotton print fabric
5/8 yard of 45"-wide cotton fabric for lining
5/8 yard of polyester fleece
One cone of decorative thread such as Supertwist, Candlelight, Glamour, pearl cotton, or Pearl Crown Rayon
Two cones of serger thread

Serger Set-Up

Decorative flatlock: Wide, 3-thread, satin-length, balanced stitch, decorative thread in upper looper and serger thread in lower looper and needle.

Seaming: Medium, 3-thread, medium-length, balanced stitch, serger thread in loopers and needle.

Instructions

1 Tear or cut 5" × 45" strips, cutting two each from cotton print and solid, one from contrast print.

2 Flatlock-piece the strips wrong sides together along lengthwise edges in following order: Cotton print, solid, contrast print, solid, cotton print (Fig. 6-6).

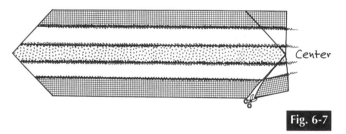

Fig. 6-6

3 Mark center at both ends of runner. At each end, cut to center mark at 45-degree angle (Fig. 6-7). Dot each end of flatlock stitching with seam sealant.

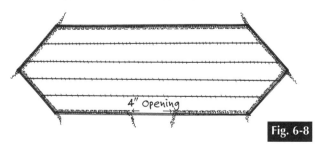

Fig. 6-7

4 Using runner as the pattern, cut lining and polyester fleece.

5 Baste fleece to wrong side of lining, close to raw edges. Place runner onto lining, right sides together. Serge-seam, leaving a 4" opening on one long side for turning (Fig. 6-8).

Fig. 6-8

6 Turn table runner right side out; press edges lightly. Slipstitch opening closed.

Mantle Scarf

Fig. 6-9

Dress up and protect your fireplace mantle with a mantle scarf. These toppers have been spotted in pricey interiors boutiques at unheard-of prices. Custom-fit and serge your own for a fraction of the price. This one sports button-trimmed ends for hanging charms and whatnots.

MATERIALS

One yard of 45″-wide lightweight print fabric for scarf
One yard of 45″-wide contrast print or solid fabric for lining
Six matching flat buttons, Three charms for trim
Two cones of decorative thread, such as Decor 6, Designer 6, or Pearl Crown Rayon
Three cones of serger thread

Serger Set-Up

Seaming: Wide, 3-thread, medium-length, balanced stitch, serger thread in loopers and needle.

Decorative edging: Wide, 3-thread, satin-length, balanced stitch, decorative thread in both loopers and serger thread in needle.

Instructions

1 Measure mantle's length and depth. Cut scarf from fabric and lining as follows, using illustration as guide (Fig. 6-10a): Width—mantle depth measurement (serging will narrow it slightly); length—mantle length measurement plus 20″ (10″ for each drop).

2 With right sides together, serge-seam scarf ends to center piece, matching straight ends (Fig. 6-10b). Repeat for lining.

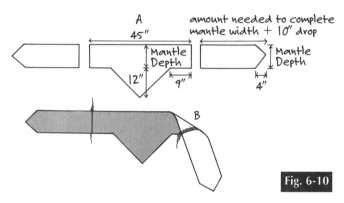

Fig. 6-10

3 Place fabric and lining wrong sides together, matching raw edges. Decoratively serge-finish all edges, taking care on inside angles (pull angle straight to serge across). Bury tail chains (Fig. 6-11).

Fig. 6-11

4 Place two buttons at each tip, sandwiching mantle scarf between each set and aligning buttonholes. Stitch through buttons, securing both from each set simultaneously. Serge off a 1/2-yard thread chain cord, using the decorative thread. Press chain to smooth. Cut chain cord into 6″ pieces, thread through charm, knot ends. Hang charms from buttons at scarf ends. (Fig. 6-12)

Fig. 6-12

Pocket Blanket

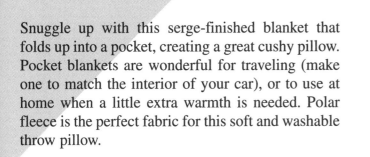

Fig. 6-13

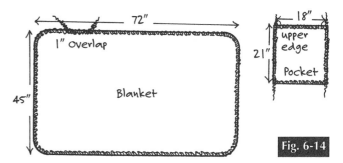

Fig. 6-14

Snuggle up with this serge-finished blanket that folds up into a pocket, creating a great cushy pillow. Pocket blankets are wonderful for traveling (make one to match the interior of your car), or to use at home when a little extra warmth is needed. Polar fleece is the perfect fabric for this soft and washable throw pillow.

MATERIALS

2 1/2 yards of polar fleece
One cone of decorative thread, such as Pearl Crown Rayon, Designer 6. Decor 6, or Janome Acrylic
Two cones of serger thread

Serger Set-Up

Wide, 3-thread, long-length, wrap stitch, decorative thread in upper looper and serger thread in lower looper and needle.

Instructions

1 From polar fleece, cut a 45″ × 72″ rectangle for blanket and an 18″ × 21″ rectangle for pocket. Round corners on blanket piece, using a large dinner plate as a guide.

2 Using decorative thread, serge-finish the blanket and pocket, overlapping stitches on blanket for approximately 1″ (Fig. 6-14). Bury tail chains.

3 Fold 3″ to right side on pocket upper edge. Topstitch close to serge-finished edge.

4 Mark center on one short edge of blanket. Mark center on pocket lower edge. With right sides up and center marks matching, pin pocket to blanket. Topstitch around outside of pocket to blanket along lower and side edges, next to serge-finished edges (Fig. 6-15).

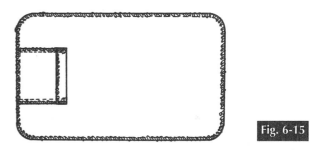

Fig. 6-15

5 To fold blanket into pocket, place blanket wrong side up. Fold blanket into thirds lengthwise, using pocket stitching as folding lines. Fold pocket inside out, flipping over end of folded blanket (Fig. 6-16a). Fold remaining end of blanket into thirds, and continue to fold into the pocket, forming pillow (Fig. 6-16b).

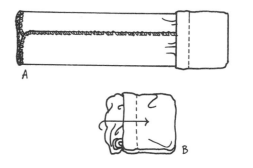

Fig. 6-16

Fig. 6-17

Lampshade Cover

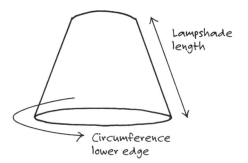

Lampshade length

Circumference lower edge

Fig. 6-18

Is the shade on your nightstand lamp looking a bit worn? Give it some new life with a cover-up serged to match your decor. Use two coordinating fabrics and a matching decorative thread to serge up this drawstring cover in a jiffy.

MATERIALS

1/2 yard of 45"-wide lightweight print fabric (more if making cover for a large lampshade—check measurement instructions below)
1/4 yard of 45"-wide coordinating, lightweight print or solid fabric
One yard of 1/4"-wide satin ribbon
One cone of decorative thread such as pearl cotton, Pearl Crown Rayon, Glamour, or Candlelight
Two cones of serger thread

Serger Set-Up

Decorative serging: Wide, 3-thread flatlock, short-length stitch, decorative thread in upper looper, serger thread in lower looper and needle.

Seaming: Wide, 3- thread, medium-length, balanced stitch, serger thread in loopers and needle.

Instructions

1 Measure lampshade's height and lower edge circumference. Add 4" to height measurement to determine cover fabric width. Add 2" to circumference to determine cover fabric length. Cut cover from print fabric, using these dimensions. Cut lower flange from coordinating fabric, 5" × cover fabric length (Fig. 6-18).

2 Press under 2" twice on one long edge of cover. Decoratively flatlock along fold, without trimming edge, catching all three layers. Pull flatlock hem open gently and press. Press flange in half lengthwise, wrong sides together. Flatlock flange to long raw edge of cover piece, wrong sides together. Pull flatlock open gently and press flange (Fig. 6-19).

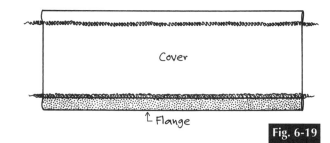

Cover

Flange

Fig. 6-19

3 With right sides together, serge-seam remaining raw edges of cover. With seam to center back, mark upper edge of center front cover. Using a small safety pin, thread ribbon under flatlock stitches, beginning and ending at center front, forming a drawstring casing (Fig. 6-20).

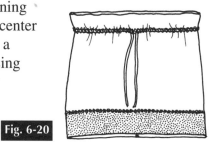

Fig. 6-20

4 Pull ribbon drawstring to fit upper rim of lampshade and tie ribbon into bow. Adjust gathers so that lampshade cover sets evenly on shade.

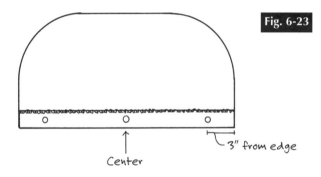

Fig. 6-21

Folding Chair Cap

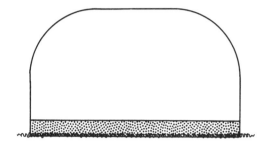

Fig. 6-22

For special occasions, dress up your folding chairs with a chair cap. This slipcover fits neatly over the top back of a standard metal folding chair and snaps to fasten. Serge-finish the outer seam with a rolled-hem stitch and contrasting decorative thread for a mock piping–edge finish.

MATERIALS

3/8 yard of decorator print fabric
1/8 yard of lightweight fusible interfacing
Three sets of decorative snaps
One cone of decorative thread, such as woolly nylon, Decor 6, or Designer 6
Three cones of serger thread

Serger Set-Up

Edge finishing: Medium, 3-thread, medium-length, balanced stitch, serger thread in loopers and needle.

Decorative seaming: 3-thread, rolled-hem, satin-length stitch, decorative thread in upper looper and serger thread in lower looper and needle.

Instructions

1 Enlarge pattern number 8 on copy machine. Cut two chair toppers from print fabric. Cut two 1 1/2″ × 20″ strips from fusible interfacing.

2 Fuse interfacing strips to wrong side of each chair topper along lower edge. Serge-finish lower edge of each piece (Fig. 6-22).

3 Press a 1 1/2″ lower edge hem allowance to wrong side of each chair topper. Mark placement of snaps on each hem 3″ from each side (raw edge, and at center. Set snaps in hem (Fig. 6-23).

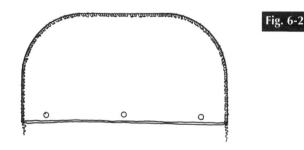

Fig. 6-23

3″ from edge

Center

4 With wrong sides together and raw edges matching, serge-seam around side/upper edges using a rolled edge. Dot seam sealant on tail chains, let dry, then trim (Fig. 6-24).

Fig. 6-24

5 Slip chair cap over back of folding chair and snap in place. Consider serging these in any fun fabric to match the festivities, such as holiday prints, garden prints, or hobby motifs.

CHAPTER 7

Just For Fun

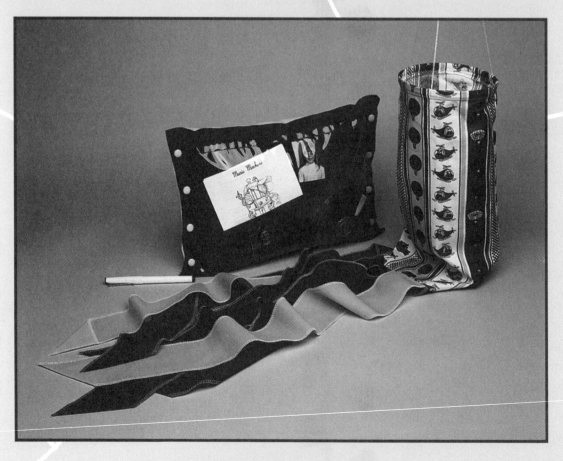

Serger Windsock

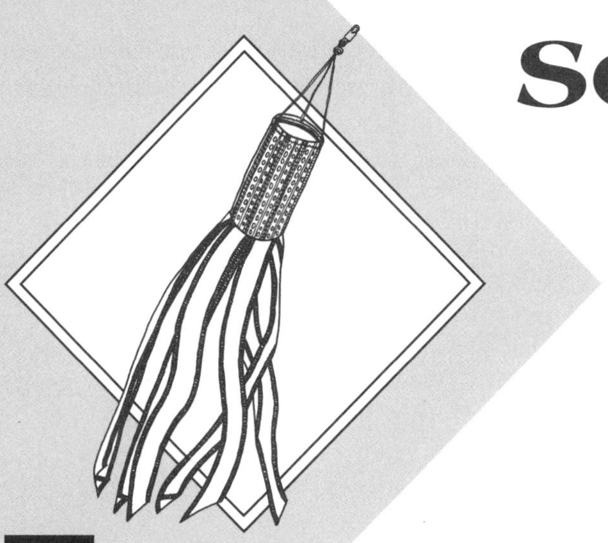

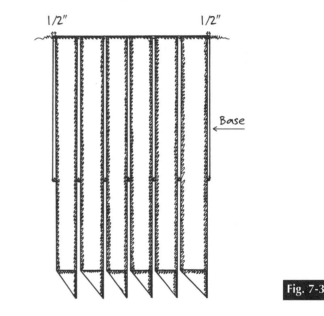

Fig. 7-1

Windsocks are bright and cheerful when blowing in the breeze on a windy day. Serge this classic design for a fun outdoor decoration that's sure to get attention. These also look neat hanging in a kid's room, especially when serged in primary colors.

MATERIALS

1/2 yard of 45"-wide lightweight cotton print or solid fabric for windsock base
1/4 yard each of lightweight cotton fabrics in three different colors/prints for tails
1/2 yard of boning
Three yards of heavy thread, such as carpet-upholstery thread, pearl cotton, or other strong fine cord
One large swivel hook (available in fishing department of sporting goods store)
One small eyebolt (available in hardware store)
Three cones of serger thread or woolly nylon

Serger Set-Up

Medium, 3-thread, medium-length, balanced stitch, serger thread or woolly nylon in loopers and needle.

Instructions

1 Cut a 16" × 18" base from windsock base fabric and two 3" × 28" tails from each tail fabric.

2 Serge-finish one long edge of a 3"-wide strip. Fold one end at a 45-degree angle, then serge opposite long side, serging through both layers at end. Dot end with seam sealant, let dry, and trim. Repeat with remaining five tails (Fig. 7-2).

Fold

Fig. 7-2

3 Serge-finish one 18" edge of base. With base right side up, place tails side by side on base's unfinished 18" edge, with colors/prints alternating (leave a 1/2" seam allowance on each side of base). Serge across edge, catching in all tail ends (Fig. 7-3).

Base

Fig. 7-3

4 With right sides together, serge side seam. Zigzag boning to serge-finished upper edge, lapping ends. Turn boning to inside and zigzag close to finished edge.

5 Pin-mark windsock upper edge into thirds. Cut heavy thread or cord into three one-yard pieces. Fold cord piece in half and thread both raw ends through eye of a large, sharp tip tapestry needle. Poke needle through upper edge at marking, just below stiff boning edge. Put needle through loop end of cord and pull taut, forming a slip knot. Repeat at other two markings (Fig. 7-4).

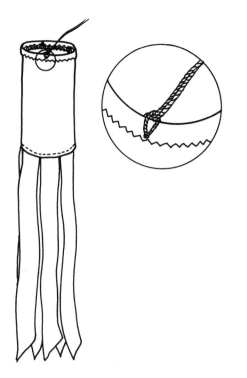

Fig. 7-4

6 Tie cord ends to swivel hook. Knot ends twice and dot knot with seam sealant to secure. Hang from eyebolt in a breezy place!

NOTE: If your windsock will get a lot of sun exposure, treat finished windsock, including cords, with a weatherproofing spray to help prevent fading and to resist moisture.

Keepsake Autograph Pillow

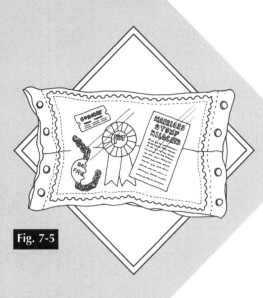

This pillow is a favorite of kids. The clear pocket displays mementos, and the reverse side of the pillow can be autographed with a permanent marker. Snaps serve as side closures for easy removal of the insert pillow. Serged in school colors, these make great gifts for the younger set.

MATERIALS

1/3 yard of solid color poplin
1/4 yard of contrast color poplin
1/3 yard of 8-gauge clear vinyl
3/8 yard of lightweight solid cotton fabric (for insert pillow)
10 ounces of polyester fiberfill
Eight sets of decorative snaps
Three cones of serger thread
Pinking shears or paper edgers

Serger Set-Up

Medium, 3-thread, medium-length, balanced stitch, serger thread in loopers and needle.

Instructions

1 From solid poplin, cut 11″ × 18″ rectangle for back. From contrast poplin, cut two 6″ × 18″ rectangles for front. From the clear vinyl, cut an 8″ × 13″ window/pocket. From lightweight cotton fabric, cut one 14″ × 22″ rectangle for insert pillow.

2 Serge-finish one long edge of each front piece. Right sides together and serged edges matching, straight stitch pillow fronts together next to serging, leaving a 6″ opening (Fig. 7-6). Press seam to one side.

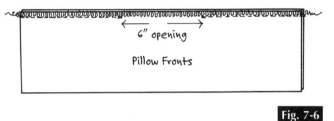

6″ opening

Pillow Fronts

Fig. 7-6

3 Trim vinyl pocket edges with pinking shears or paper edgers. Center pocket on pillow front right side, then topstitch 1/4″ from all edges (Fig. 7-7).

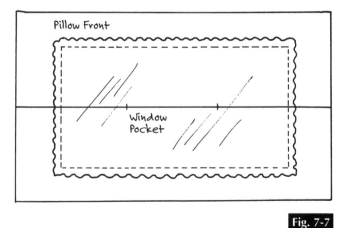

Pillow Front

Window Pocket

Fig. 7-7

4 With right sides together, serge-seam pillow front and back along one long edge. Press seam to one side. Serge-finish side edges. Press under 1 1/4″ side hems, unfold hems, then serge-seam remaining long edges right sides together. Turn right side out.

5 Fold hems under, then topstitch close to serge-finished edge (Fig. 7-8).

6 Finish pillow "case" by placing and setting four snaps on each end, spacing evenly (refer back to Fig. 7-5).

7 For insert pillow, fold rectangle in half crosswise, wrong sides together, and serge-seam two sides. Fill with fiberfill, then serge remaining side closed.

Place mementos through opening on case wrong side. Place insert pillow inside "case" and close snaps. Use fine-line permanent marker to autograph back of pillow.

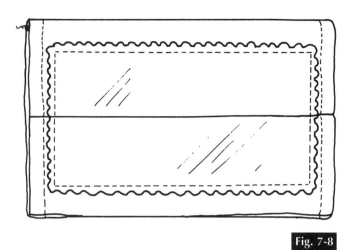

Fig. 7-8

Quilt-Block Banner

Fig. 7-9

Flatlocking makes fast and easy serging of this quilt-block-inspired banner. Jewel-toned fabrics and black woolly nylon thread give this banner a stained-glass look. Hang indoors with a dowel rod and ribbon or outside with a flag/banner pole.

MATERIALS

1/3 yard each of three different lightweight cotton fabrics
1/3 yard of lightweight cotton fabric, same as one of fabrics above, for casing
Three cones of woolly nylon
3/4" dowel rod, 32" long, for indoor display

Serger Set-Up

Block piecing: Medium, 2- or 3-thread flatlock, satin-length stitch, woolly nylon in loopers and needle.

Edge finishing: Medium, 3-thread, satin-length, balanced stitch, woolly nylon in loopers and needle.

Instructions

1 From each fabric cut two 5"-wide strips, the length of the fabric's width.

2 Flatlock-piece three strips together (use one strip of each color) along lengthwise edges (Fig. 7-10). Repeat to create an identical flatlocked panel. Pull flatlocking open gently and press.

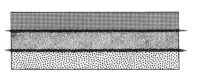

Fig. 7-10

3 From each flatlocked panel, cut two 14 1/2" squares. Flatlock squares back together as shown in illustration (Fig. 7-11).

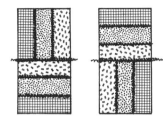

Fig. 7-11

4 Cut a 5" × 29" strip from casing fabric. Serge-finish both long edges of casing strip, then serge-finish upper edge of flatlocked-pieced banner block. Lap one long edge of casing over banner upper edge and topstitch close to serge-finished edge. Serge-finish sides and lower edge of banner (Fig. 7-12).

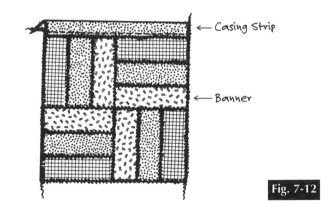

← Casing Strip

← Banner

Fig. 7-12

5 Wrap casing edge over banner upper edge to the wrong side. Topstitch in place along previous stitching line. Bury tail chains.

To display indoors, place finished banner on dowel rod and hang, using narrow satin ribbon or cord tied to each end. For outdoor display, treat banner with weatherproofing spray to protect from sun and moisture, then place on flag/banner pole.

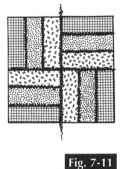

Toss-It Game

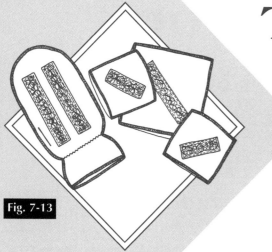

Fig. 7-13

Kids will have lots of fun with this bean bag game of catch. Learning how to toss and catch will be a breeze for young children because of the Velcro on the rice-filled bags and catcher's mitt. Since older kids like to keep score, the three different size/type bags are assigned point values; the player with most points wins the game.

MATERIALS

1/4 yard of Lycra knit fabric for bags
1/4 yard of polar fleece for mitt
7" of 1/4"-wide elastic
1 yard of 3/4" sew-in Velcro
8 cups of rice (not instant variety)
Three cones of woolly nylon

Serger Set-Up

Narrow, 3-thread, short-length, balanced stitch, woolly nylon in loopers and needle.

Instructions

1 Using pattern number 9, cut two mitts from polar fleece. From Lycra, cut four 5" squares and eight 4" squares.

2 Attach Velcro to right side of all pieces. On one mitt, stitch two 5" strips of Velcro, loop side, 3" from lower edge as shown. On two 5" Lycra squares, center and stitch a 5" piece of Velcro, hook side, diagonally as shown. On two 4" squares, center and stitch a 4" Velcro piece, hook

side, diagonally as shown. On two 4" squares, stitch a 1" Velcro piece, hook side, in one corner diagonally, within edges (Fig. 7-14).

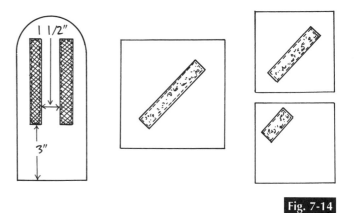

Fig. 7-14

3 Zigzag a 3 1/2" piece of elastic on the wrong side of each mitt according to pattern marking, stretching elastic to fit. Cut a 2"-long thumb slit on "Velcro-ed" mitt 4" from lower edge, 1/2" from outer edge (make slit close to left edge for left-handed catcher, on right edge for right-handed catcher). See Figure 7-15.

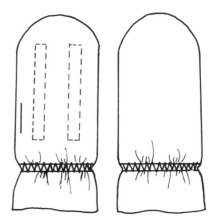

Fig. 7-15

4 With wrong sides together and raw edges matching, serge-seam mitt pieces around side and top edges. Bury tail chains.

5 Place one "Velcro-ed" Lycra square on same-size plain square wrong sides together;

serge-seam three edges, repeating until six bags are serged. Fill each 5″ bag with 2 cups of dry rice and each 4″ bag with 1 cup. Pin each bag closed, 1″ from raw edge, placing pins vertically and close together, to keep rice from seeping out of bag. Serge-seam each bag closed (Fig. 7-16). Dot all bag corners with seam sealant, let dry, and trim.

Have child place mitt on hand with thumb through slit. Velcro makes catching tossed bags easier for small children. To play, two players take turns, one tossing and one catching, until six bags are tossed, then players trade places. Catcher earns points for each bag caught: 1 point for each large bag, 2 points for small bag with long Velcro strip, 3 points for small bag with short Velcro strip. Play two or more rounds. Player with the most points at the end of the game wins.

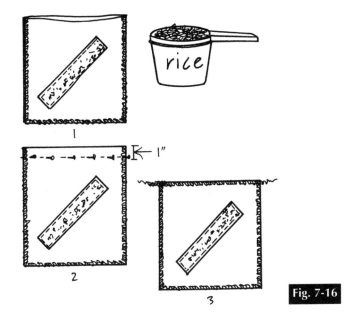

Fig. 7-16

Bike Pouch

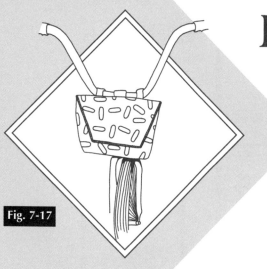

Fig. 7-17

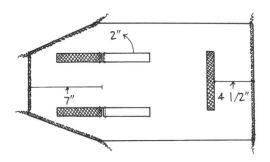

Fig. 7-18

Stow all kinds of gear in this quick-serged bike pouch. Attach to handlebars with durable Velcro tabs. This is a must-have item for bikers young and old alike. Kids especially like these and will want you to serge them for all of their friends!

MATERIALS

1/3 yard of lightweight cotton print fabric
1/3 yard of HeatNBond Lite
11" of Velcro
Three cones of serger thread or woolly nylon

Serger Set-Up

Narrow, 3-thread, short-length, balanced stitch, serger thread or woolly nylon in loopers and needle.

Instructions

1 Enlarge pattern number 10 on photocopy machine. Cut two pouches from fabric and one from HeatNBond. Fuse HeatNBond to wrong side of one pouch. Place pouches wrong sides together; fuse, forming one reversible piece.

2 Serge-finish upper edge, upper sides, and lower edge. Stitch 5" Velcro strip, hook side, 4 1/2" from lower edge. Place 3" Velcro strips on pouch, hook and loop ends opposite each other, with ends 7" from upper edge and 2" in from each outside raw edge as shown (Fig. 7-18). Stitch ends only.

3 Fold bottom portion of pouch in half crosswise, right sides together, and serge side seam. Stitch 5" Velcro strip, loop side, to inside upper edge of flap, centering between finished sides (Fig. 7-19a). Box or miter lower corner, stitching 1" from folded point. Turn bag right side out (Fig. 7-19b).

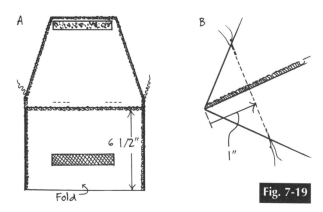

A

B

6 1/2"

1"

Fold

Fig. 7-19

4 Place pouch on handlebars by wrapping Velcro "loop" strip over handlebar, then lapping "hook" strip onto "loop" strip, fastening tabs tightly (Fig. 7-20).

Fig. 7-20

CHAPTER

8

Giftables

Video Box Cover

Fig. 8-1

A serged box cover is a pretty way to display a special video. Serge this cover from memorable fabrics and trims, such as bridal satin and lace for a wedding video, pink or blue prints for a baby video, juvenile motifs for a kid's video—you get the idea! Decorative threads finish edges for a nice touch.

MATERIALS

1/3 yard each of two lightweight fabrics for cover and lining
1/3 yard of fusible fleece
Lace edging, appliqués, or decorative trims of your choice
3" strip of 3/4"-wide Velcro
One cone of decorative thread, such as RibbonFloss, Designer 6, Decor 6, Pearl Crown Rayon, or Janome Acrylic
Three cones of serger thread

Serger Set-Up

Decorative edge finishing: Medium, 3-thread, satin-length, balanced stitch, decorative thread in upper looper and serger thread in lower looper and needle.

Seaming: Medium, 3-thread, medium-length, balanced stitch, serger thread in loopers and needle.

Instructions

1 Enlarge pattern number 11 on photocopy machine. Cut a box cover from fabric, lining, and fleece. Fuse fleece to wrong side of fabric. Place prepared fabric and lining wrong sides together. Baste all around close to edges (Fig. 8-2).

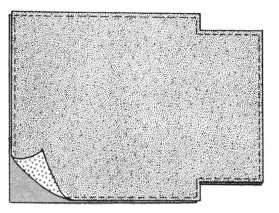

Fig. 8-2

2 With right side facing up, decoratively serge-finish flap edges and corners, and opposite edge as shown. Embellish as desired. For cover shown, lay two pieces of lace edging on cover diagonally, with a serge-finished strip of contrast fabric through center of edging; top-stitch in place (Fig. 8-3).

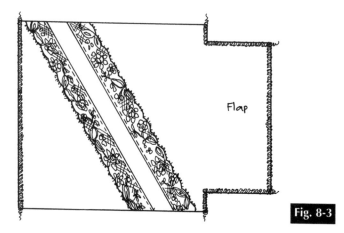

Flap

Fig. 8-3

3 Machine stitch Velcro, hook side, to right side of box cover according to pattern marking. Center and hand stitch or fabric glue Velcro, loop side, to inside edge of flap.

4 Fold bottom portion of box cover in half crosswise, right sides together, matching side seam raw edges. Serge side seams and bury tail chains (Fig. 8-4a). Box/miter corners, stitching 1/2" from folded point. Trim off excess at corners (Fig. 8-4b).

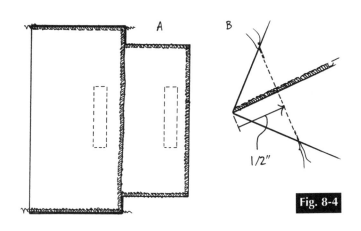

A   B

1/2"

Fig. 8-4

5 Turn cover right side out. Insert video tape box and fold flap over to fasten.

Fifteen-Minute Gift Bags

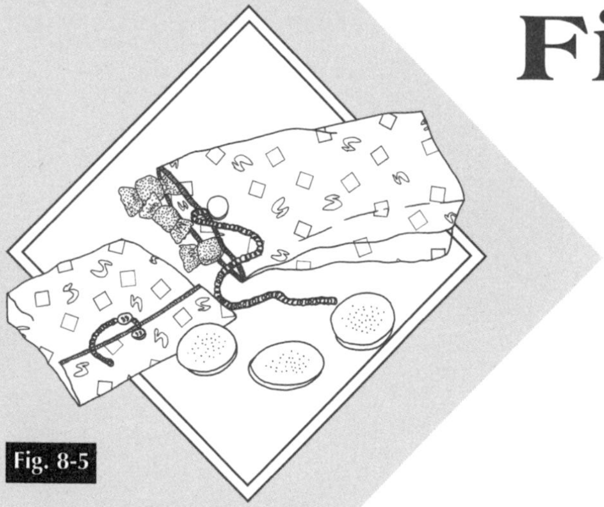

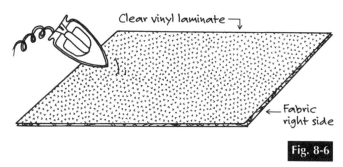

Fig. 8-5

These bags are a practical and pretty alternative to traditional wrapping paper. Serge a cookie bag using fusible fabric laminate as the liner, or laminate the outside for a reusable, wipe-clean bag. Cheerful cotton prints combined with decorative threads and stylish buttons make these bags a treat to give and receive.

MATERIALS

Cotton print fabric: 1/2 yard for 10″ × 11″ cookie bag; 1/3 yard for 8″ × 7″ gift bag
HeatNBond Flexible Iron-On Vinyl: 1/2 yard for cookie bag, 1/3 yard for gift bag
One cone of decorative thread, such as Candlelight, Glamour, Reflection, Ribbon Floss, or Pearl Crown Rayon
Three cones of serger thread
Two buttons

Serger Set-Up

Decorative edge finishing: Narrow, 3-thread, satin-length, balanced stitch, decorative thread in upper looper and serger thread in lower looper and needle.

Seaming: Narrow, 3-thread, medium-length, balanced stitch, serger thread in loopers and needle.

Instructions

1 For cookie bag, cut one 14″ × 22″ rectangle from fabric and laminate; for gift bag, cut one 12″ × 14″ rectangle from fabric and laminate.

Fuse laminate to wrong side of cookie bag fabric and to right side of gift bag fabric, following manufacturer's instructions (Fig. 8-6). Save backing paper to use as a press cloth on right side of laminated surface.

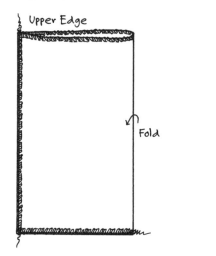

Clear vinyl laminate

Fabric right side

Fig. 8-6

2 Decoratively serge-finish one long edge (upper edge), then fold piece in half, right sides together. Serge-seam bottom and side edges (Fig. 8-7).

Upper Edge

Fold

Fig. 8-7

3 Box/miter lower edges, stitching 1″ from folded point (Fig. 8-8). Turn bag right side out. With press cloth (or backing paper from Iron-On Vinyl), press side edges and crease boxed bottom so bag will stand up. Fold over top edge of bag 2″ and press.

4 Chain off 12″ of decorative thread for chain cord for each bag. Stitch buttons on through

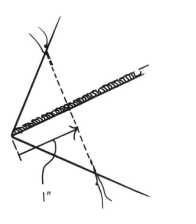

Fig. 8-8

one layer close to foldover edge, then beneath foldover on body of bag. Tie cord end around base of button on flap. Knot other end of cord, dot both knots with seam sealant, let dry, and trim. To close bag, twist cord around both buttons, in a figure eight, wrapping around base of buttons loosely two or three times (refer back to Fig. 8-8).

Book/Bible Cover

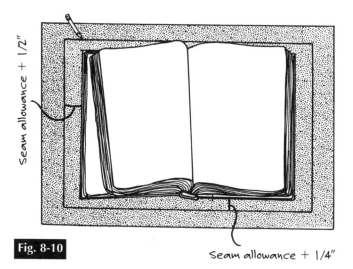

Fig. 8-9

Protect a favorite book or bible with this padded cover featuring convenient carrying handles. Custom-size each cover to your needs, using some simple measurements. You can serge these in large sizes too to fit binders or datebook.

MATERIALS

NOTE: To figure yardage, measure book, bible, or notebook open-width and length (upper to lower edge).

45"-wide lightweight cotton print fabric for cover, lining, and inside flaps: Twice open book length measurement plus 4"
45"-wide coordinating lightweight cotton print fabric for pocket and handles: Open book length measurement plus 12"
Polyester fleece: Open book length measurement
HeatNBond Lite: Three times open book length measurement
Paper to make pattern
Two cones of decorative thread, such as woolly nylon, woolly nylon metallic, or fine rayon
One cone of serger thread

Serger Set-Up

Narrow width, 3-thread, satin-length, balanced stitch, decorative thread in loopers and serger thread in needle.

Instructions

1 Make pattern by opening book out flat on paper. Measure open width and length (upper to lower edge), adding seam allowances all around, plus 1/4" at upper and lower edges and 1/2" at side edges for ease. Cut pattern using these dimensions (Fig. 8-10).

Fig. 8-10

Seam allowance + 1/2"

Seam allowance + 1/4"

2 Fuse HeatNBond to wrong side of cover, lining and flaps fabric, and pocket and handles fabric, covering surface completely. Cut each fused fabric in half crosswise. Fuse fleece to wrong side of one half of cover/lining/flaps fabric, then fold fused fabric wrong sides together, with fleece sandwiched between, fuse to form padded fabric. Repeat for pocket/handles fabric. From cover/lining/flaps padded fabric, cut two covers using paper pattern (refer back to Fig. 8-10). Fold paper pattern in half crosswise, making pocket pattern. From pocket/handles fabric, cut one pocket from padded pocket fabric. Cut handle piece twice open book length plus 16", 4" wide, from padded pocket fabric.

3 To make the two inside flaps, cut one padded cover piece in half lengthwise. Serge-finish one long edge of each flap, both long edges of pocket, and all edges of handle piece (Fig. 8-11).

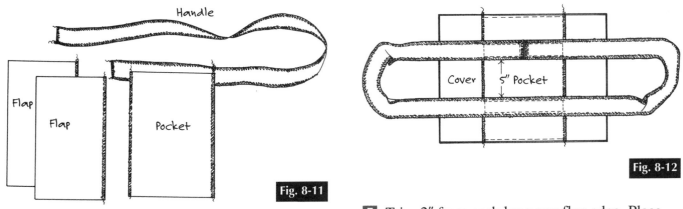

Handle

Flap

Flap

Pocket

Fig. 8-11

Cover   5" Pocket

Fig. 8-12

4 Center pocket on right side of book cover and baste close to raw edges. Stitch handles on pocket area of cover/pocket, starting at pocket center, with 5″ between straps as shown, and leaving 8″ loop at each end for handles (Fig. 8-12).

5 Trim 2″ from each long raw flap edge. Place flaps on cover wrong side, one on each end, matching raw edges. Serge-seam through all layers on all sides of cover. Optional: To make narrow handles, fold handle loops in half, matching finished edges. Stitch close to finished edges, as shown in Figure 8-9.

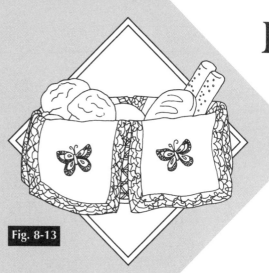

Fig. 8-13

Heirloom Bread Basket Liner

Add a Victorian touch to your table setting with this bread basket liner trimmed in delicate lace. Heirloom serging techniques, combined with lightweight batiste, create that light and airy look for this easy-to-serge table linen. These make great hostess gifts—serge several at the same time.

MATERIALS

1/4 yard of cotton batiste fabric
3 1/2 yards of 3/4"-wide heirloom lace edging
Four appliqués
One spool of fine rayon thread
Two cones of serger thread

Serger Set-Up

Narrow, 3-thread, rolled-hem, medium-length stitch, fine rayon thread in upper looper and serger thread in lower looper and needle.

Instructions

1 Cut two 6" × 18" rectangles of batiste.

2 Roll-hem all edges of each rectangle. Dot corners with seam sealant, let dry, and trim (Fig. 8-14).

Fig. 8-14

3 Place rayon thread on sewing machine and set for narrow-width, medium-length zigzag stitch. On one hemmed piece, right side up, place straight edge of lace trim over rolled edge and zigzag trim right along edge (lace should just hide rolled hem; do not overlap too much). At each corner, fold lace at right angle, zigzag out to point, trim excess lace from back of fold, then turn and continue onto next edge, mitering each corner. Repeat with remaining hemmed piece (Fig. 8-15).

Fig. 8-15

4 Pin-mark center of each lace-trimmed piece. With right sides up, stack as shown, matching centers to form a crisscross. Using rolled hem as guide, straight stitch a "box," securing rectangles together (Fig. 8-16).

Fig. 8-16

5 Tack one appliqué at each end of liner. Place liner in bottom of round or square bread basket and drape ends over sides of basket.

NOTE: The liners can be made without the lace trim from any kind of lightweight print fabric. Try edging rectangular pieces with pretty decorative threads before stitching together.

Growth Chart

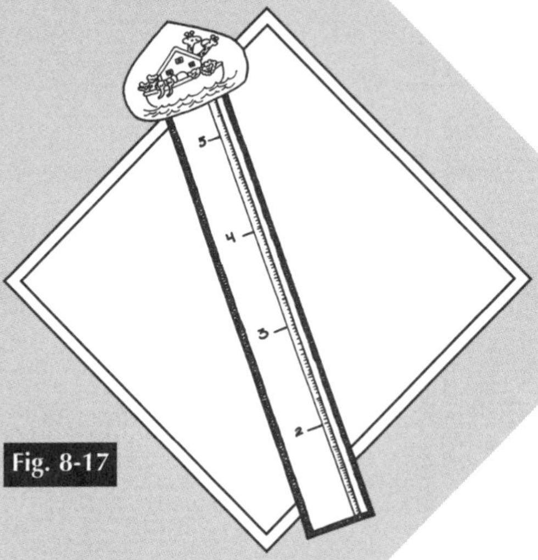

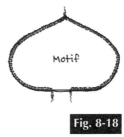

Fig. 8-17

Kids seem to grow like weeds. To keep track of their growth, chart it on this cute wall hanging. Use a permanent marker to note date and height on the attached measuring tape, as a lasting history for both parent and child. This makes a perfect gift for a child's first birthday.

MATERIALS

1/4 yard of 60"-wide medium-weight woven fabric
6" square of juvenile-motif print fabric
1/4 yard of 60"-wide lightweight cotton fabric for lining
1/4 yard of lightweight fusible interfacing
4 1/2 yards of 5/8"-wide satin ribbon with ruler print, cut so that measurements start at 1"
Fabric paint, Fabric glue
Polyester fiberfill, approximately 4–6 ounces
One cone of decorative thread, such as Ribbon Floss, Pearl Crown Rayon, or pearl cotton
Three cones of serger thread, Permanent fabric marker

Serger Set-Up

Seaming: Medium width, 3-thread, medium-length, balanced stitch, serger thread in loopers and needle.

Decorative edging: Medium width, 3-thread, satin-length, balanced stitch, decorative thread in upper looper and serger thread in lower looper and needle.

Instructions

1 From lining and juvenile print, cut a loose shape, following contours of the motif and adding a bit for seam allowances. Cut one 4" × 52" strip from medium-weight fabric and interfacing. Fuse interfacing to wrong side of strip.

2 With right sides together, serge-seam motif to lining, leaving opening to turn for stuffing (Fig. 8-18). Turn right side out, then stuff lightly with fiberfill. Slipstitch opening closed.

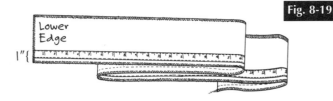
Motif
Fig. 8-18

3 Place ribbon on right side of fabric strip, 1" from long right-hand edge. Make sure ribbon is positioned so measurements read from bottom to top. Edgestitch ribbon in place. Decoratively serge-finish both long edges and lower short edge of fabric strip (Fig. 8-19).

Fig. 8-19
Lower Edge
1"{

4 Chain off 6" for a decorative-thread chain loop. Fold in half, then center and topstitch to upper edge of finished strip as shown on left side of Figure 8-20.

5 Glue padded motif to strip upper edge, covering chain loop ends. Fabric paint a number at each foot mark, leaving room between for written dates as shown on right side of Figure 8-20. Use a permanent fabric marker to note growth marks.

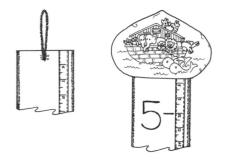
Fig. 8-20

CHAPTER

9

Celebrations

Pretty Packages Appliquéd Sweatshirt

Fig. 9-1

Embellish a sweater or sweatshirt with appliquéd fabric "packages." Choose small Christmas prints and shiny metallic thread for holiday appeal. These make great mother-daughter matching tops and can be serged up in a snap.

MATERIALS

Ready-made sweatshirt or sweater
1/8 yard each of four coordinating holiday prints
1/4 yard of HeatNBond Lite
One spool each of metallic decorative thread and clear monofilament thread
One cone of serger thread

Serger Set-Up

Narrow, 3-thread, short-length, balanced stitch, metallic thread in upper looper, monofilament in needle, and matching serger thread in lower looper.

Instructions

1 From one print fabric, cut a 1"-wide strip the length of the fabric width. Cut three 3 1/2" squares from the remaining prints and from HeatNBond.

2 Serge-finish both long edges of 1"-wide fabric strip (Fig. 9-2).

Fig. 9-2

3 Fuse HeatNBond to wrong side of each fabric square. Cut two 3 1/2"-long pieces from serge-finished strip. With right sides up, center a 1" × 3 1/2" strip on a fabric square; repeat. Serge-finish around each square, catching in serge-finished strip (Fig. 9-3). Serge-finish remaining fabric square. Bury tail chains.

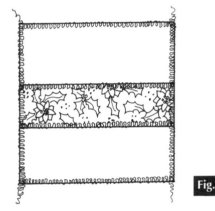

Fig. 9-3

4 Fuse finished packages on sweatshirt or sweater front, as shown on Figure 9-1. Topstitch close to serge-finished edges of each square.

5 Cut three 6"-long pieces from serge-finished strip. Fold each 1" × 6" strip in half crosswise, right sides together. Serge-seam raw ends of each, forming loop. Turn each loop right side out and center seam on underside. Chain off 1 yard of decorative thread chain. Cut chain into three 12" pieces and tie each fabric loop through center, wrapping tightly to form bow (Fig. 9-4).

Fig. 9-4

6 Place bow at center upper edge of each package. Tack through bow center. Pull bow loops upward, then tack on each side of loop close to bow center.

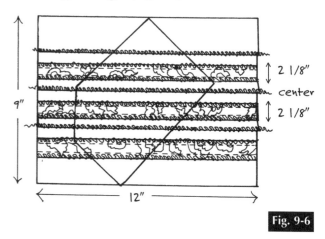
Fig. 9-5

Christmas Stocking

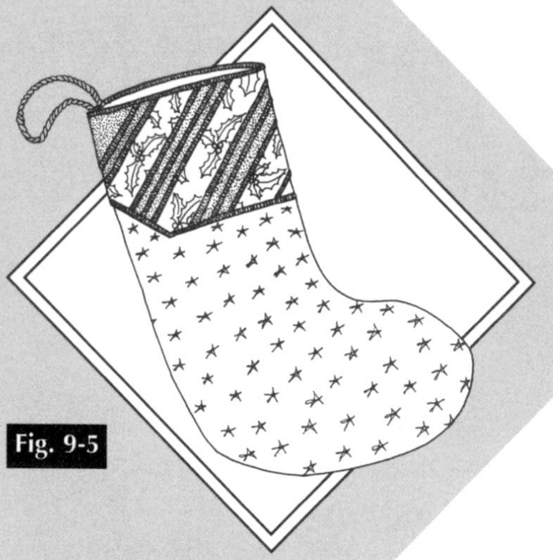

This beautiful decoratively serged Christmas stocking looks like it took hours to make. Only you will know it took a mere sixty minutes! Serged tucks and trim embellish the shaped cuff on this padded stocking. Its so easy that you can serge one for every member of the family.

MATERIALS

Three coordinating 45"-wide lightweight cotton Christmas prints:

    3/4 yard for stocking
    1/4 yard for cuff
    1/8 yard for trim

1/2 yard of polyester fleece, 1 yard HeatNBond Lite
Two cones of decorative thread, such as
    Candlelight, Glamour, or Pearl Crown Rayon
Three cones of serger thread

Serger Set-Up

Decorative rolled edge: 3-thread, rolled-hem, short-length stitch, decorative thread in upper looper and serger thread in lower looper and needle.

Decorative edge finishing: Medium, 3-thread, satin-length, balanced stitch, decorative thread in loopers and serger thread in needle.

Seaming: Medium, 3-thread, medium-length, balanced stitch, serger thread in loopers and needle.

Instructions

1 Enlarge pattern number 12 on photocopy machine. Cut four stockings from fabric (two for stocking, two for lining) and two each from fleece and HeatNBond. Using pattern number 13, cut one each from fleece and HeatNBond. Cut one 1" × 36" strip from trim fabric. Fuse HeatNBond, then fleece, to wrong side of each stocking lining.

2 Cut a 9" × 12" rectangle from cuff fabric. Mark lengthwise lines for rolled tucks on fabric right side, one through center, then one on each side of center, spacing 2 1/8" apart. Roll-hem a tuck along each line, then press tucks to one side. Roll-hem each long edge of 1" × 36" strip. Cut finished strip into three 12"-long pieces and place a finished strip between tucks and below last tuck. Topstitch strips close to each serge-finished edge. Using pattern number 13, cut one cuff from embellished fabric, turning pattern at a 45-degree angle (Fig. 9-6).

9"

2 1/8"
center
2 1/8"

12"

Fig. 9-6

3 Cut a cuff lining piece from print fabric using same pattern. Fuse HeatNBond to wrong side of cuff lining piece, then fuse fleece to lining piece. Place cuff and cuff lining wrong sides together. Decoratively serge-finish lower edge and angle of cuff. Bury tail chain. Chain off a 5" decorative-thread chain; set aside.

4 Place one stocking and one lining piece, wrong sides together for stocking front. Place wrong side of finished cuff on right side of stocking front, matching raw upper edges. Serge-finish upper edge, catching in edge of cuff on front. Place remaining stocking and lining wrong sides together for stocking back. Serge-finish upper edge (Fig. 9-7).

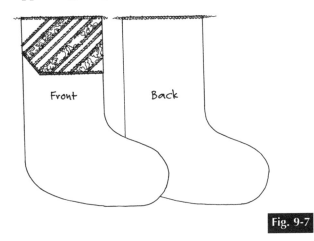

Fig. 9-7

5 With right sides together and raw edges matching, serge-seam around outer edge of front and back. Bury tail chains. Topstitch chain cord loop to inside lining, upper edge of stocking for hanging loop (Fig. 9-8).

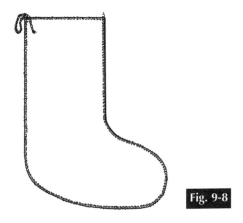

Fig. 9-8

6 Turn stocking right side out; press edges lightly.

Serged Cards and Tags

Fig. 9-9

Using shiny or metallic decorative thread, some holiday trims, and a little creative inspiration, you can serge gift cards and tags. Friends and family love to receive these and will admire you for your cleverness!

MATERIALS

Blank cards with matching envelopes (available in craft and stationary stores)
Scraps of holiday print fabric, HeatNBond Lite, and heavyweight fusible interfacing
Lace trim, Fabric glue, Paint pen/marker
One spool of metallic embroidery thread
Two cones of decorative thread, such as Glamour, Candlelight, Pearl Crown Rayon, or Ribbon Floss
Two cones of serger thread

Serger Set-Up

Edging cards: Wide, 3-thread, satin-length, balanced stitch, decorative thread in upper looper and serger thread in lower looper and needle.

Tags: Wide, 3-thread, satin-length, balanced stitch, decorative thread in loopers and serger thread in needle.

SERGED CARDS

Instructions

1 Measure width of lace trim. Cut this amount from lower front edge of card, then decoratively serge-finish this edge (do not trim paper with serger blade). Bury tail chains, dot with seam sealant, and trim neatly. With card open, glue lace under serge-finished edge (Fig. 9-10).

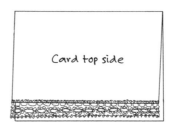

Card top side

Fig. 9-10

2 Fuse interfacing to wrong side of piece of holiday fabric. Embroider message to fit on card front. Cut fabric in shape to fit card, serge-finish edges, bury tail chains, and glue to card front. Optional: Use paper edgers or pinking shears to trim edge of envelope flap.

SERGED TAGS

Instructions

1 Cut approximately 3″ × 4″ or larger rectangles from holiday print fabric and HeatNBond. Using HeatNBond, fuse two fabric pieces wrong sides together. Serge-finish fabric and bury tail chains (Fig. 9-11).

Fig. 9-11

2 Using paint pen, write message on tag or on pretrimmed paper glued to tag. Using decorative thread, chain off a 6″ cord. Place chain through large, sharp tip tapestry needle, thread through corner of tag, knot loose ends, and trim (Fig. 9-12).

TO: MOM
FROM: ANN

Fig. 9-12

Elegant Serged Ornaments

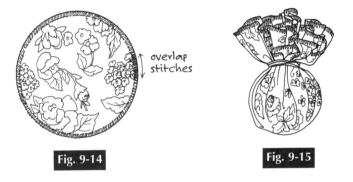

Fig. 9-13

Make elegant ornaments from foam balls and cotton prints serged with glistening decorative threads. Holiday and decorator fabrics, button charms, flower picks, and ribbon trim add the finishing touch. Serge one of several variations, like the "carnation" top, created by doubling up the pretty serge-finished circles.

MATERIALS

1/2 yard of 45"-wide lightweight holiday or decorator print fabric (makes three to four ornaments)
3" Styrofoam balls (one for each ornament)
Two cones of decorative thread, such as Sulky Sliver, Supertwist, or Sulky Metallic
One spool of clear monofilament thread or one matching cone of serger thread
Decorative charms, small flower picks
Fishline, Straight pins, Small rubber bands

Serger Set-Up

Medium, 3-thread, satin-length, balanced stitch, decorative thread in loopers and clear monofilament or serger thread in needle.

Instructions

1 Cut one 14" circle of print fabric for each ornament (two if doing "carnation" top—see "Variations" below).

2 Decoratively serge-finish each circle, overlapping stitches slightly. Bury tail chains (Fig. 9-14).

3 Place foam ball in center of wrong side of serge-finished circle. Hand-gather edges up and secure with rubber band. Adjust gathers so fabric is tight around foam ball and finished edges are even (Fig. 9-15).

↑ overlap stitches

Fig. 9-14

Fig. 9-15

4 To make ribbon, cut a 3/4" × 6" (approximately) fabric strip. Decoratively serge-finish both long edges. Cut piece in half, loop charm through one piece, and straight-pin raw ends of loop at base of rubber-banded gathers, into foam ball. Starting at back of ornament, wrap remaining piece around gathers, covering rubber band and raw edges of loop. Overlap at back, trim excess, and use straight pin to secure into foam (Fig. 9-16).

Fig. 9-16

5 For loop hanger, cut a 7" piece of clear fishline. Fold in half, forming loop; knot ends. Use straight pin to secure knotted end of loop through center of gathers into foam ball.

Variations

Instead of a charm, use a flower pick inserted in center of gathers into foam ball. Use satin ribbon or decorative cord to cover rubber band in lieu of serged ribbon. For an extra-full "carnation" top, use two serge-finished circles and gather as described above. Adjust gathers, separating layers for a full look.

Fig. 9-17

Easter Gift Basket

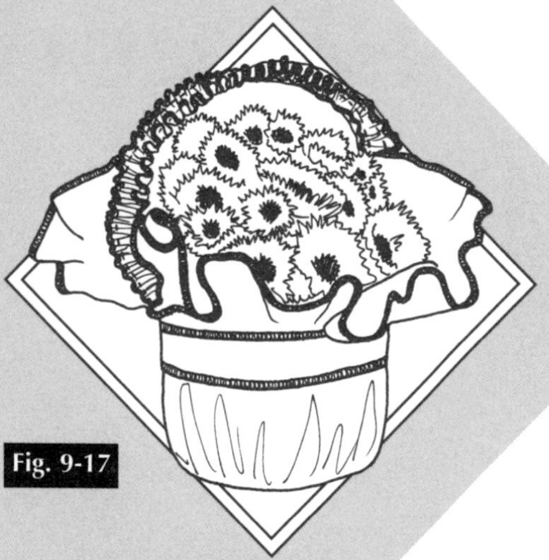

edges of each strip. On 45″-long strip, stitch 1/2″ from each serge-finished edge, forming center casing. Bury tail chains on circle (Fig. 9-18).

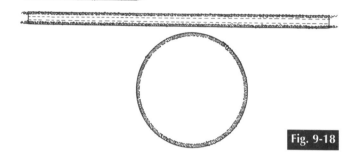

Fig. 9-18

Recycle a plastic margarine container into this lovely Easter basket. Some cheery springtime fabric, decorative threads, and fabric stiffener combine to create this unique serged gift. Fill with pretty flowers and give a friend (or yourself) a beautiful Easter treat.

MATERIALS

3/4 yard of lightweight cotton springtime print fabric
3-pound margarine container, empty and washed
One 12″ × 18″ sheet of heavyweight plastic canvas
One bottle of spray fabric stiffener, such as Stiffen Stuff
Two brass brads (available in office supply stores)
Large rubber band to fit around upper edge of margarine container (may substitute 1/4″-wide clear elastic, ends tied together)
Two cones of decorative thread, such as Sulky Rayon, Sulky Metallic, Supertwist, or Ultrasheen
One cone of serger thread

Serger Set-Up

Medium width, 3-thread, satin-length, balanced stitch, decorative thread in loopers and serger thread in needle.

Instructions

1 From fabric, cut two 20″ circles, one 3″ × 20″ strip, and one 5″ × 45″ strip.

2 Place circles wrong sides together, and press strips in half lengthwise, wrong sides together. Decoratively serge-finish circle and both long

3 Protect work surface with newspaper. Place margarine container upside down, elevating on a tall drinking cup or coffee can. Center finished fabric circle over container. Use large rubber band to secure circle to container, rolling rubber band to upper edge and adjusting gathers evenly. Spray covered container with fabric stiffener until soaked. Dry with hair dryer, shaping gathered edge as desired. Repeat spray stiffener application and dry cycle as many times as needed to achieve stiff basket. Pin-fit 20″-long serge-finished strip around upper edge of basket. Remove and serge-seam ends, right sides together, for a band (Fig. 9-19).

Fig. 9-19

4 Cut a 1″ × 18″ strip of plastic canvas. Insert it through casing on 45″-long strip, gathering strip onto canvas. Stitch close to ends to secure shirred ruffle to plastic canvas strip, creating basket handle. Mark sides of basket approximately 1″ down from upper edge. Use pointed scissors to poke small hole at each side. Place a brad through each end of handle, then through holes on basket. Open brads, pressing tight against plastic container. Cover brad ends with clear tape if desired (Fig. 9-20).

5 Slide band back onto basket, covering handle ends and rubber band, adjusting if needed to achieve a very snug fit. Place potted flower in container, or use a block of florist foam to secure silk flowers in basket.

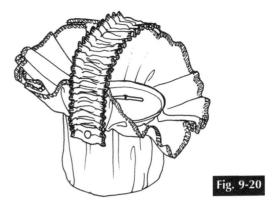

Fig. 9-20

All-Occasion Candle Rings

Fig. 9-21

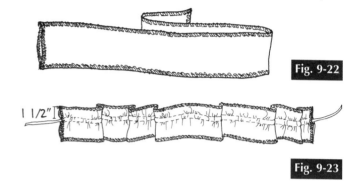

Fig. 9-22

Fig. 9-23

Dress up a plain candlestick with these super-easy candle rings. Choose different fabrics and decorative threads for each, creating several different looks. Clear elastic makes sizing simple. Add the serged tassel for a fashionable decorator look.

MATERIALS

1/4 yard of 45"-wide lightweight fabric for each candle ring

Three cones of decorative thread, such as Sulky Metallic, Sulky Rayon, Supertwist, or Ultrasheen

12" of 1/4"-wide clear elastic

3" cardboard square

Serger Set-Up

Decorative edging: Medium, 3-thread, satin-length, balanced stitch, decorative thread in loopers and needle.

Tassel: Narrow, 3-thread, rolled-hem, satin-length stitch, decorative thread in loopers and needle.

Instructions

1 Square up edges of 9" × 45" fabric piece. Decoratively serge-finish both short ends, then fold in half lengthwise, wrong side together. Decoratively serge-finish each long edge. Bury tail chains (Fig. 9-22).

2 Stitch 1 1/2" from one long edge, then again 1/2" below that, to form casing. Thread clear elastic through casing (Fig. 9-23).

3 Pull gathers tight and tie elastic so candle ring fits loosely around base of candlestick. Trim elastic ends. Adjust gathers evenly.

4 Chain off approximately 6 yards using rolled-hem and decorative thread. Wrap chain thirty times around cardboard square. Thread a 12" piece of chain through upper fold, tie loose knot, and slide off of cardboard. Tie knot tight and cut bottom loops. Wrap another 12" piece of chain around top of tassel, tie ends and trim. Trim tassel ends even (Fig. 9-24).

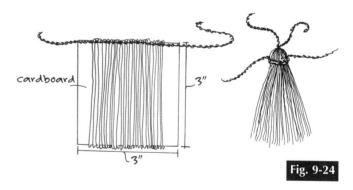

cardboard

3"

3"

Fig. 9-24

5 Tie tassel to elastic at center opening of candle ring.

PATTERNS

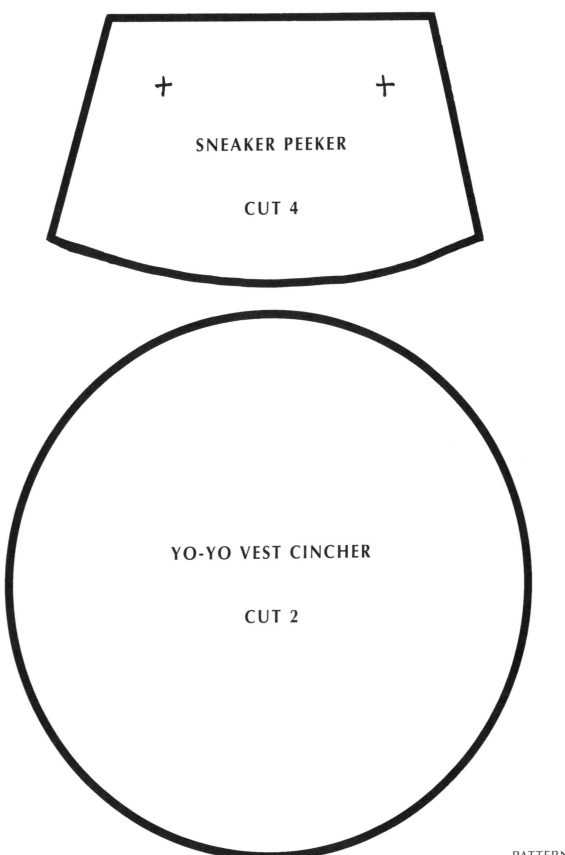

SNEAKER PEEKER

CUT 4

YO-YO VEST CINCHER

CUT 2

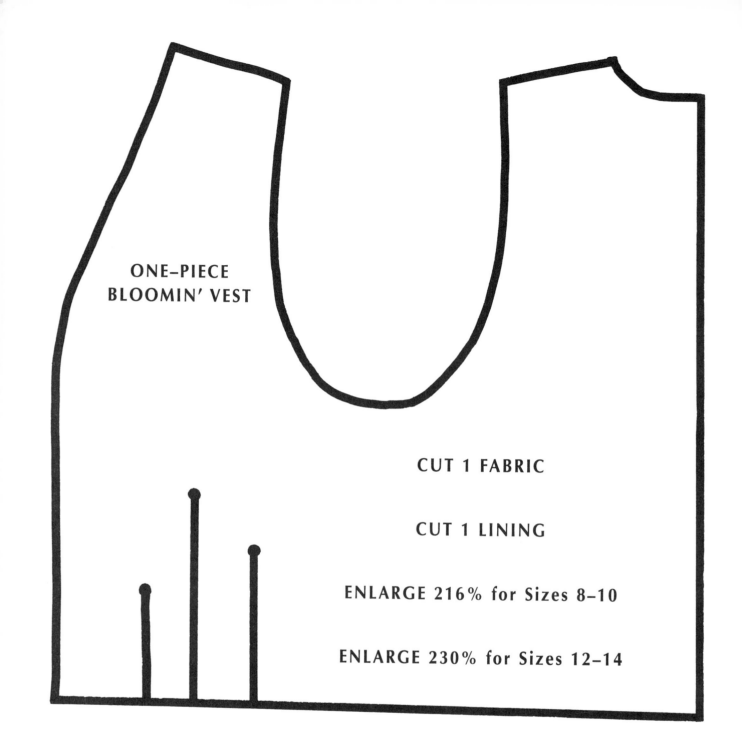

ONE–PIECE
BLOOMIN' VEST

CUT 1 FABRIC

CUT 1 LINING

ENLARGE 216% for Sizes 8–10

ENLARGE 230% for Sizes 12–14

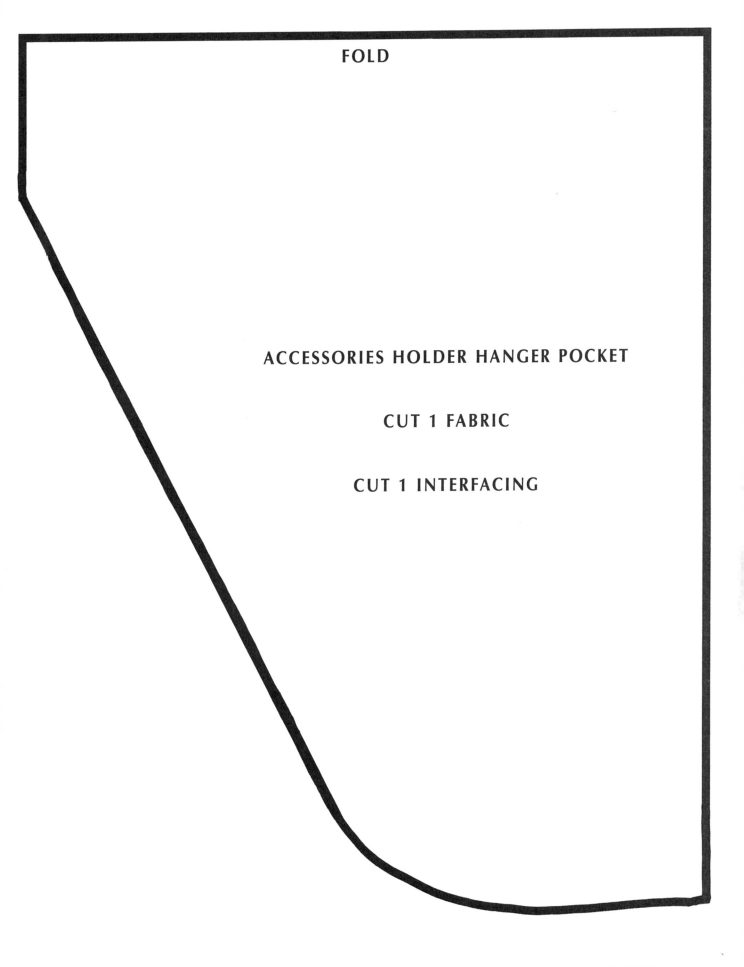

FOLD

ACCESSORIES HOLDER HANGER POCKET

CUT 1 FABRIC

CUT 1 INTERFACING

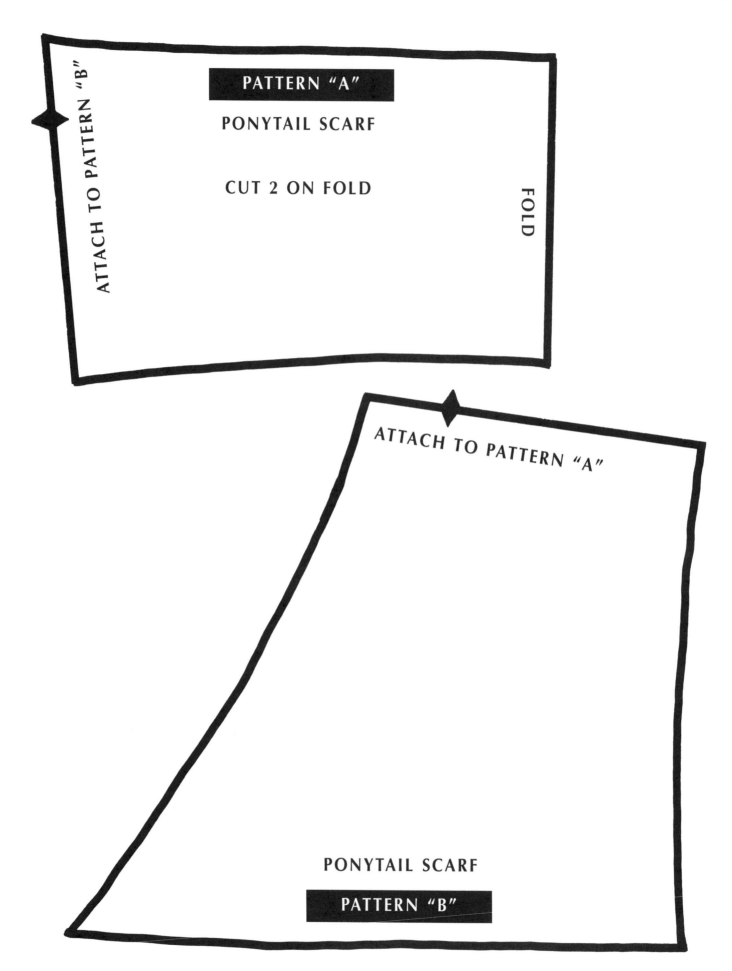

PATTERN "A"

PONYTAIL SCARF

CUT 2 ON FOLD

ATTACH TO PATTERN "B"

FOLD

ATTACH TO PATTERN "A"

PONYTAIL SCARF

PATTERN "B"

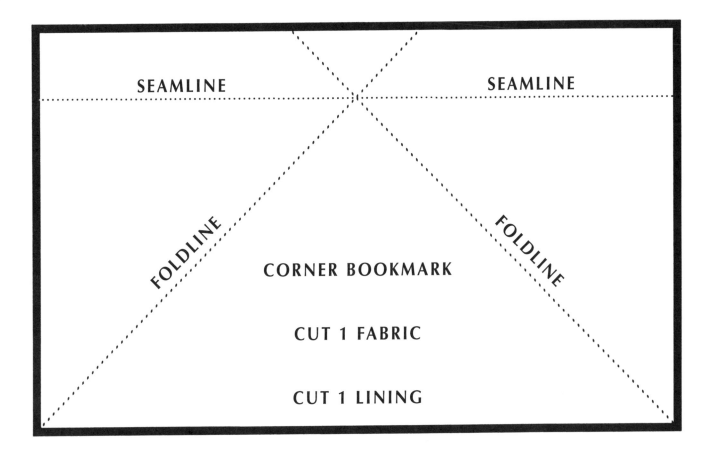

SEAMLINE   SEAMLINE

FOLDLINE   FOLDLINE

CORNER BOOKMARK

CUT 1 FABRIC

CUT 1 LINING

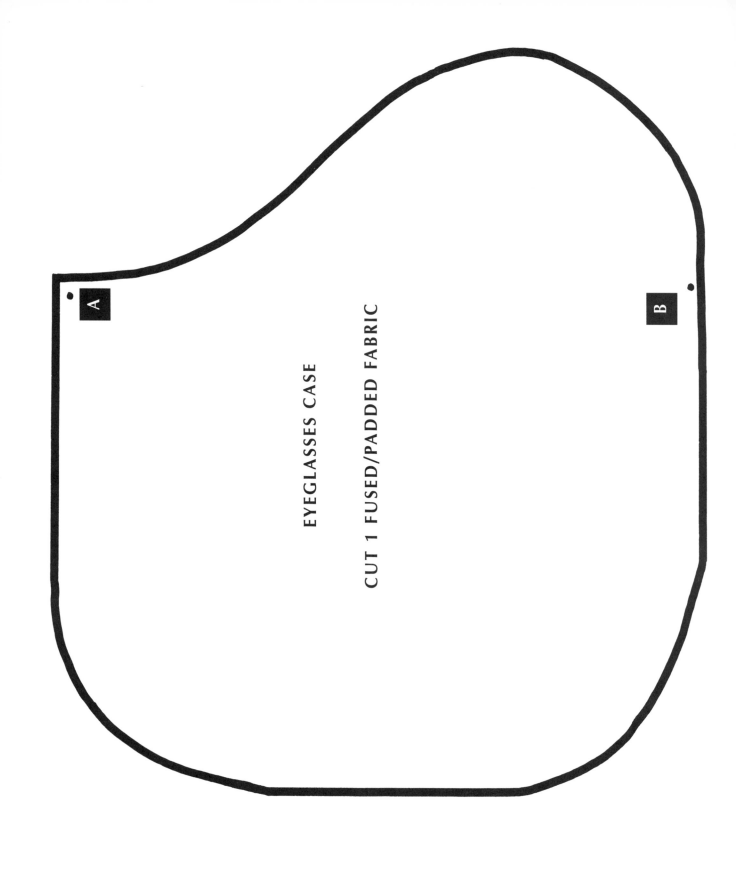

A

B

EYEGLASSES CASE

CUT 1 FUSED/PADDED FABRIC

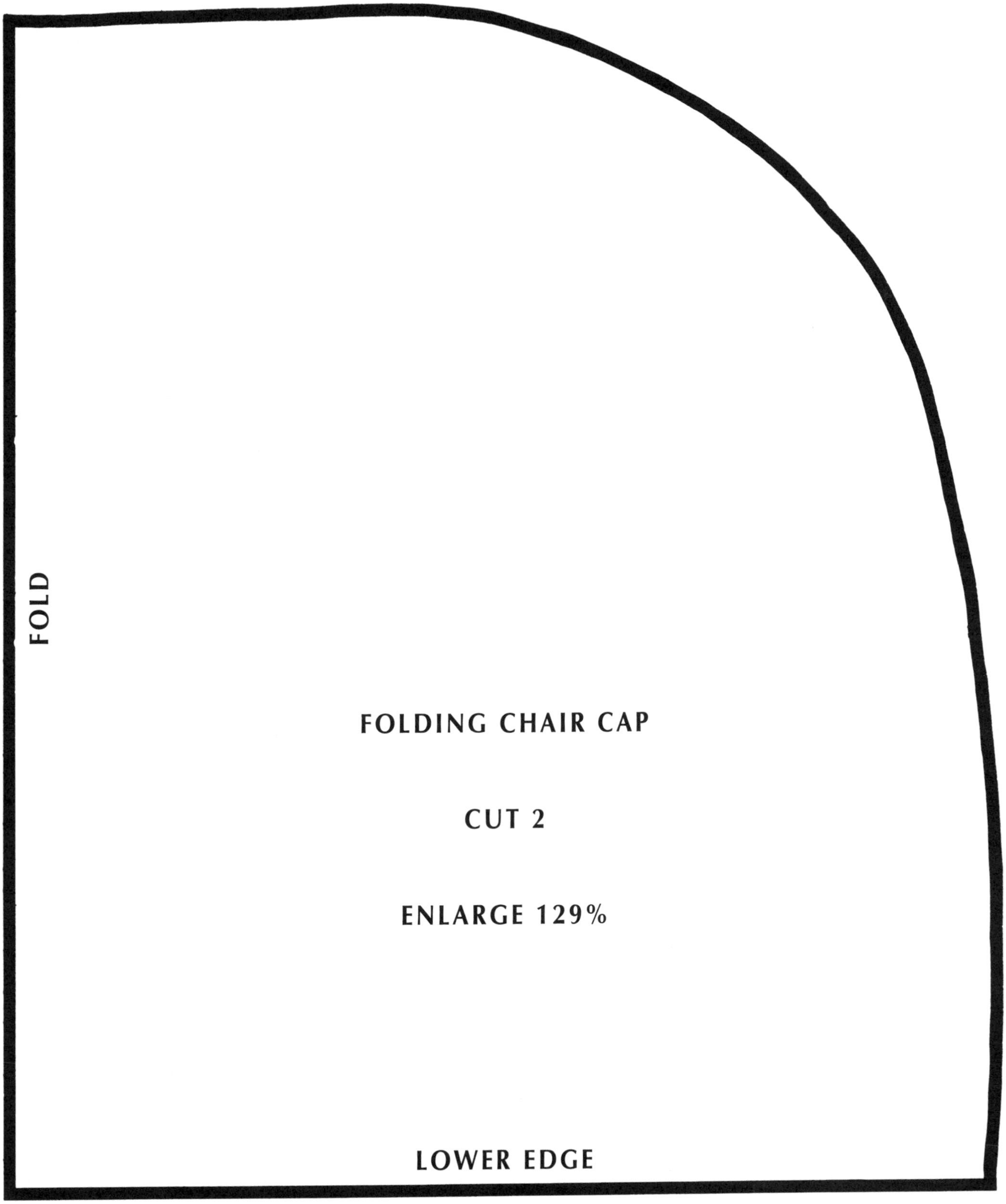

FOLD

FOLDING CHAIR CAP

CUT 2

ENLARGE 129%

LOWER EDGE

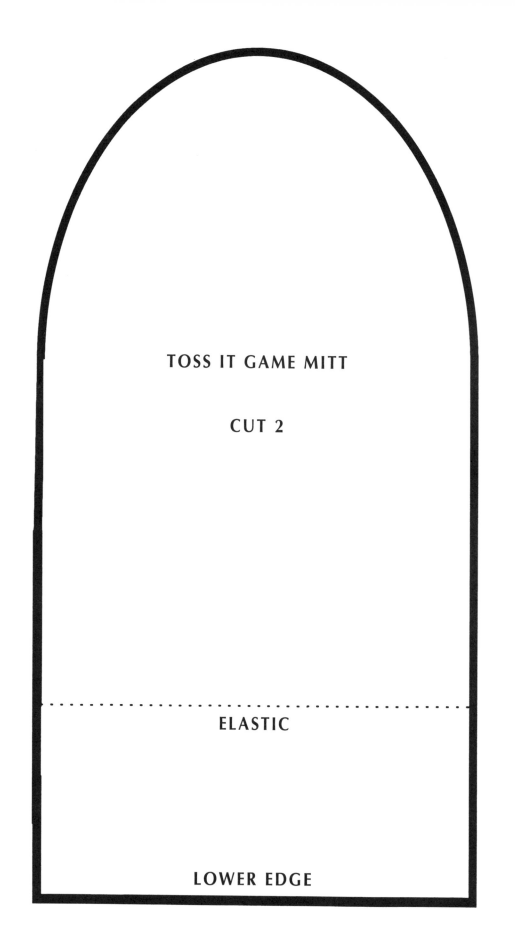

TOSS IT GAME MITT

CUT 2

....

ELASTIC

LOWER EDGE

BIKE POUCH

CUT 1 FABRIC

CUT 1 LINING

CUT 1 FUSIBLE ADHESIVE

ENLARGE 205%

FLAP AREA

VELCRO HOOK

VIDEO BOX COVER

CUT 1 FABRIC

CUT 1 LINING

CUT 1 FUSIBLE FLEECE

ENLARGE 142%

FLAP

VELCRO LOOP

CHRISTMAS STOCKING

CUT 2 FABRIC

CUT 2 LINING

CUT 2 FUSIBLE FLEECE

ENLARGE 189%

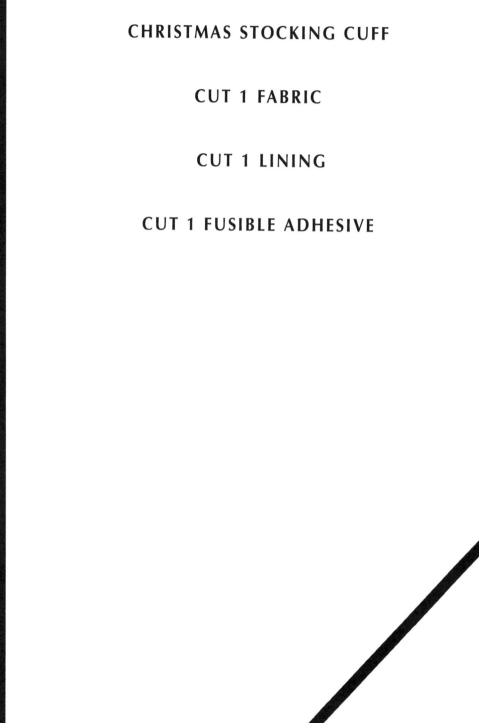

CHRISTMAS STOCKING CUFF

CUT 1 FABRIC

CUT 1 LINING

CUT 1 FUSIBLE ADHESIVE

LOWER EDGE

RESOURCES

FABRICS

Fabrics from these companies were used for several projects in this book. Look for them at your favorite fabric retailer. If you have difficulty locating them, contact the manufacturer for assistance.

CAPITOL IMPORTS, INC.
P.O. Box 13002
Tallahassee, FL 32317
(800) 521-7647

Cotton batiste, heirloom lace trim (Heirloom Bread Basket Liner)

CONCORD FABRICS
1359 Broadway
New York, NY 10018
(800) 223-5678

Cotton holiday prints (Christmas Stocking, Elegant Serged Ornaments, Serged Cards and Tags)

FABRI-QUILT INC.
901 E. 14th Ave.
N. Kansas City, MO 64116
(816) 471-2853

Juvenile cotton print (One-Piece Bloomin' Vest), cotton print (Mantle Scarf)

JOHN KALDOR FABRICMAKER
500 Seventh Ave., 10th Floor
New York, NY 10018-4502
(212) 221-8270

Polyester silk-look, cotton print (Video Box Cover), cotton prints (Book/Bible Cover)

PINE CREST FABRICS
4831 N.E. Freemont
Portland, OR 97213

Polar fleece (Easy-Fit Headband), interlock (Sunburst Bead-Trimmed Tee)

PRINCESS FABRICS
1040 Sixth Ave.
New York, NY 10018
(800) 223-5900

Juvenile motif (Growth Chart)

STYLETOWN FABRICS
35 W. 35th St.
New York, NY 10001
(212) 695-0140

Juvenile print (Serger Windsock)

V.I.P FABRICS
1412 Broadway
New York, NY 10018
(212) 730-4600

Cotton prints (Quilt-Block Banner, Fifteen-Minute Gift Bags, Easter Gift Basket, All-Occasion Candle Rings)

PRODUCTS

These products were used for creating several of the projects in this book. Ask for these at your local retailer. If you need assistance in locating a product, contact the manufacturer for retailer information.

BEACON CHEMICAL COMPANY
125 MacQuesten Parkway South
Mount Vernon, NY 10550
(914) 699-3400

Fabri Tac fabric glue, Stiffen Stuff fabric stiffener, and other related products

BIRCH STREET CLOTHING
P.O. Box 6901
San Mateo, CA 94403
(415) 578-9729

Vario Plus Snap Kit and specialty children and adult patterns; $1.00 for catalog

C.M. OFFRAY & SON, INC.
P.O. Box 601, Rte. 24
Chester, NJ 07930
(908) 879-4700

Ruler ribbon, loads of pretty ribbons and trims. Check local retailer, or call for dealer location information

CLOTILDE, INC.
2 Sew Smart Way
Stevens Point, WI 54481
(800) 772-2891

Clear elastic, Horizontal Thread Holder, and related sewing and serging notions; free catalog

THE CROWNING TOUCH, INC.
2410 Glory C Rd.
Medford, OR 97501
(503) 772-8430

FASTURN fabric tube turner, related sewing patterns and products; $1.00 for color catalog

FISKARS, INC.
Wausau Business/Creative Works
7811 W. Stewart Ave.
P.O. Box 8027
Wausau, WI 54402-8027
(715) 842-2091

Paper edgers, rotary cutters, shears, and related notions

HANDLER TEXTILE CORPORATION
24 Empire Blvd.
Moonachie, NJ 07074
(800) 666-0335

Line of interfacings, fleece, and related products

JHB INTERNATIONAL, INC.
1955 S. Quince St.
Denver, CO 80231
(303) 751-8100

Angel charms (Elegant Serged Ornaments, Mantel Scarf), cord lock (Water Bottle Tote), a beautiful line of buttons, buckles, clips, etc.

NANCY'S NOTIONS
333 Beichl Ave.
P.O. Box 683
Beaver Dam, WI 53916
(800) 833-0690

Needle/looper threaders, double-eyed needle, lots of sewing and serging notions; free catalog

SPEED STITCH
3113 Broadpoint Dr.
Harbor Heights, FL 33983
(800) 874-4115

Sulky Tear Easy (Keepsake Autograph Pillow, Accessories Holder, Notions Wall Hanging), lots of decorative threads and related products; catalog

THERM O WEB
770 Glen Ave.
Wheeling, IL 60090
(800) 992-9700

HeatNBond Lite (Five Triangles Appliquéd Sweatshirt, Bike Pouch), HeatNBond Flexible Iron-On Vinyl (Fifteen-Minute Gift Bags, Serger Thread Catcher)

VELCRO USA, INC.
P.O. Box 5218
Manchester, NH 03108
(603) 669-4892

Sew-in 1″-wide Velcro (Bike Pouch, Video Box Cover, Serger Thread Catcher), Velcro Sticky Back 1″-wide tape (Serger Thread Catcher)

THREADS

These companies supplied threads used for several of the projects in this book. Look for their products at your local retailer. If you have difficulty locating them, contact the manufacturer for assistance.

A & E THREAD MILLS
P.O. Box 507
Mount Holly, NC 28120
(704) 827-4311

Maxi-Lock cone serger thread, Signature sewing thread, Swiss Metrosene sewing and serger threads, and YKK zippers

COATS & CLARK
P.O. Box 24998
Greenville, SC 29616
(803) 234-0331

Serging and sewing threads, including pearl cotton

ELNA, INC.
7642 Washington Ave. S.
Eden Prairie, MN 55344
(800) 848-3562

Ribbon Thread, 100% rayon. Call for dealer location information

MADEIRA USA
30 Bayside Ct.
Laconia, NH 03246
(800) 426-3641

Specialty threads, in larger put-ups, including Decor 6, Decor 12, and others. Especially for cottage industry; catalog

MADEIRA DIV./SCS USA
9631 N.E. Colfax
Portland, OR 97220-1232
(800) 547-8025

Decorative serger threads, including Decor 6, Glamour, and lots of other sewing and serging-related threads and notions; color catalog

NEW HOME SEWING MACHINE COMPANY
10 Industrial Dr.
Mahwah, NJ 07430
(800) 631-0183

Janome Acrylic embroidery thread, 100% acrylic heavy decorative thread. Call for dealer location information

PFAFF AMERICAN SALES
P.O. Box 566
Paramus, NJ 07653
(800) 526-0273

100% Rayon Mez Alcazar embroidery thread, 100% polyester Supersheen construction/embroidery thread. Call for dealer location information

RHODE ISLAND TEXTILE CO.
P.O. Box 999
Pawtucket, RI 02862
(401) 722-3700

Ribbon Floss and Reflection Metallic Braid

SOURCE MARKETING, LTD.
600 E. 9th St.
Michigan City, IN 46360
(219) 873-1000

GlissenGloss, couching threads, and other fiber products

SULKY OF AMERICA
3113 Broadpoint Dr.
Harbor Heights, FL 33983
(800) 874-4115

Sulky Rayon, Sulky Metallic, Sulky Sliver, Sulky 100% Polyester Clear Monofilament; color catalog

WEB OF THREAD
3125 Lone Oak Rd.
Paducah, KY 42003
(502) 554-8185

Specialty serging threads, including Burmilana, FS Jewel, and Supertwist. Sewing threads, yarn, ribbon, and cords for the needle artist; color catalog

YLI, INC.
P.O. Box 109
Provo, UT 84603
(800) 854-1932

Pearl Crown Rayon, woolly nylon, Designer 6, Success Acrylic Serging Yarn, Jeans Stitch, and lots of threads and related notions; color catalog

GLOSSARY

Balanced stitch—A serger stitch is balanced when the upper and lower looper tensions are adjusted so the threads meet on the very edge of the fabric, forming loops. The loops should hug the edge of the fabric, not fall off the edge or create a tunnel effect from incorrect tension settings.

Clean-finish—Similar to serge-finish; use a balanced 3- or 4-thread stitch to finish the edge of one layer of fabric while cutting off a scant amount of the fabric edge. Sometimes referred to as "cleaning up the edge" of the fabric. Usually used to finish edges before or during construction process.

Clear stitch finger—This procedure is used for many serging techniques. Raise the presser foot and the needles. Pull some slack in the needle threads above the needle eye, then gently pull the fabric to the back of the machine, sliding stitches off of the stitch finger (refer to your machine manual to identify the stitch finger on your serger).

Decorative thread—Any thread of contrasting color, weight, or texture used for decorative purposes. A wide variety of decorative threads are available for serger use.

Flatlock—A special stitch used for seaming, whereby when the finished seam is pulled gently open, the seam lays flat. Also for decorative effects. Tension settings are adjusted, and may be a 2- or 3-thread stitch. (See Serger Review, page xi.)

Rolled hem—Can be an edge finish or a seam. Sometimes called a narrow rolled edge. May be a 2- or 3-thread stitch. Tension settings are adjusted so that the raw edge of the fabric rolls to the back side. (See Serger Review, page xi.)

Serge-finish—Using a balanced 3- or 4-thread stitch to finish the edge of one layer of fabric. May be decorative or functional.

Serge-seam—Using a balanced 3- or 4-thread stitch to seam two layers together. Usually a medium width and medium length stitch is used.

Serger thread—Thread made specifically for serger sewing; it is cross-wound on cones so that it feeds evenly off the top of the cone during high-speed sewing. This thread is finer or lighter than all-purpose thread and is manufactured in a variety of fiber contents. The most common serger thread for general-purpose serging is 100% polyester.

INDEX

ABOUT THE AUTHOR

Cindy Cummins works and lives at her home office/studio in O'Fallon, Missouri, with her husband, Steve, and their two children, Allyce and Jonathan. With a B.S. in Clothing and Textiles from Northeast Missouri State University, she worked in retail and corporate sales for several years before returning to her first love and passion—sewing. Cindy is the designer of the "Coat in a Day" serger pattern, author of *Serge Something Super for Your Kids* (Chilton Book Company, 1994), and a contributing writer and columnist for *Serger Update* newsletters and *Sew News magazine.*
   You can write to Cindy at:

The Cutting Edge
P.O. Box 70
O'Fallon, MO 63366
email: sergecindy@juno.com